D1630627

YOUR BAND IS A VIRUS!
Expanded Edition
by
James Moore
The ultimate marketing guide for serious,
independent musicians and bands.

www.independentmusicpromotions.com

Table of Contents

INTRODUCTION

Welcome to "Your Band is a Virus – Expanded Edition". If you are reading this for the first time, or perhaps if you read the original edition, it means you've decided to take a chance on a different kind of music marketing book, or e-book. Why is it different? An industry mogul or pundit did not write this book. I am an independent promoter, and I am always learning. The goal of the "Your Band Is a Virus" series is to share what has worked for me after much trial and error. If you take even a portion of the advice in this book to heart, it could save you years of wasted time.

The idea behind the title "Your Band Is a Virus" is a mindset. If you can turn on that mindset and get inspired, yet neutral, about promoting your band, you are on the right track and this will help you with the work that's ahead.

And you can bet there will be work. Let's be realistic. If you're not enthused about working hard to expose your music to more people, no one else will be. You may as well stay in your room and play your acoustic if you're not willing to log the hours, because otherwise, you are confusing a hobby with a profession, and in the process creating unnecessary conflict in yourself and in the world. This is important to understand. The difference between a hobby and a profession is simply where the effort and intent is directed.

Legendary record producer Stuart Epps once told me that, when Elton John was on the road to fame, it took him and a team of over fifty people working around the clock to make this happen. That woke me up as to what it actually takes behind closed doors. This is for someone who already had developed his immense talent and image, and did the work of gathering a team of professionals around him. I make this point simply to give a dose of perspective.

[3]

Much of this expanded edition, besides providing a host of new tactics with which to work with, will be addressing the number one issue affecting independent musicians today; the issue of perspective. Somewhere along the line, the image of the rock star affected our culture so deeply, that it became one of the most desired and lusted after professions imaginable. But somewhere along the line, we also bought into all the services that were sold to us in order to play up this deep-seeded desire.

We bought into the automated "submit your music" type services. We bought into the "get your music in front of 10,000 journalists" automated press release schemes. We bought into endless fly-by-night managers and promotion companies who barely lifted a finger. We bought into the illusion that if we record a song and post it on our social networks, that we are entitled to earn a profit on it. We bought into the idea that if we just made good music, people would find us. And many of us sacrificed the quality and passion of our art itself in order to appeal to this industry, only serving to lower public expectations in the process. This series of rude awakenings and rejections has left us cynical and closed-off to new ideas. When someone suggests licensing our music, we say "I'm not selling out." When festivals are recommended, we say "I don't agree with the submission fees." Instead of properly promoting our music, we post it on Bandcamp and say "we're DIY", as if that truly means anything without action.

To varying degrees, in life and in our approach to what we hope to achieve, we find ourselves heavily polarized. These polarities conflict with each other, creating constant contradiction and tension even when we're unaware of it. Our deep-seeded ideas, no matter how convenient they may be, effectively hold us in place, and we achieve nothing. I think the time has come to approach music making, music marketing, and life itself from a space of open-mindedness, neutrality, and spaciousness rather than a set of pre-formed conclusions. There is no single way, only your way, and everything is possible. So get ready to start building your band's public profile in a big way.

Your Band is a Virus:

Every product, art piece, or idea in our modern society can be related to this concept. This means that while an idea or product can certainly spread quickly amongst the general public, some methods are much more effective than others. Spam, for example, is an advertising method that many potential customers have built up immunity to, and it is therefore a poor choice to utilize for bands trying to promote themselves. That's not to say that it didn't work at one time, but it's utterly ineffective now.

The goal for the independent musician is to find creative ways to get more and more people to "catch" their virus, and also to create multiple avenues for the virus to spread with ease. As I promote, I call the process "planting seeds". If you plant enough good seeds and tend to them with great care, some of them will grow beyond your wildest expectations. It takes time and energy, but if the music is strong and heavy effort is put in, people will heed the call.

In "Your Band Is A Virus – Expanded Edition", I will attempt to provide something not offered by many other "Independent band guides" or "Independent marketing e-books". It's going to be in plain English. More killer. Less filler.

Now I'm not out to name any names here, but have you purchased or read many other music marketing e-books?

How many cartoons did you see taking up half the space of the respective books? Chances are the images of someone madly typing away at a keyboard didn't help you much with your promotional efforts, right? I figured that.

The main issue I see in a lot of the musician's guides, whether they are in book form, or blog form is a general vagueness that fails to address enough actionable steps. Many times the marketing advice blogs are posted solely for SEO (search engine optimization) purposes, and the books are put out innocently enough with an old school mindset. I've read the same books in my search for the best tactics to promote with. Some books are filled with story after story – "Band 'A' from New York decided to send out free chocolate bars (or insert other item that you would NEVER in a million years send) with their promo packages."

(This story could take up three pages as you search it frantically for relevance to your own band.)

While this style of writing can definitely provide some helpful ideas and get the creative process going, it can also be somewhat insulting to pay for a marketing book, and finish it with very little to work with as far as real-life scenarios. It's quite similar to attending a weekend motivational or financial seminar and realizing on Sunday evening that you didn't actually learn anything useful.

We know that what works for a pop artist will simply not work for a death metal band. An acoustic performer can perform at the local bookstore, but the hard-core punk band cannot. Therefore, there's simply no need for a book filled solely with examples, particularly ones regarding giving out sweets of any kind. I assume that you are all creative people and you will have no trouble thinking of more powerful and compelling ways to put the ideas in this book to good use.

That being said, this edition will include a special series of industry interviews, where I ask the critical questions that are on the minds of independent musicians to experts in music production, marketing, licensing and radio, to name a few. I'll also be profiling the winners of last year's Sonicbids competition and discussing why the chosen artists stood out to me. On top of this, I'll be adding just about every effective marketing tip I can find to this book in the hopes of filling it with more than an artist could possibly use. I'm selling the farm, so to speak. Consider it a giant workbook. Don't expect a linear path.

It's the philosophy and the thinking behind independent music marketing, and success, for that matter, that needs to change. Independent musicians have reduced themselves to a horde of spammers, unable to communicate with their potential fan bases or tap into modern marketing practises. To prove this point, when was the last time you checked out a band that sent you an email saying "Check us out!" or "Saw you were a fan of (insert band name here). Thought you would like our stuff"? I`m sure you never have. Perhaps you were invited ten separate times to a live event happening half way across the globe? This is desperation marketing at work, although the bands themselves don't realize it.

So to any of you bands who just realized that this fits your description to a tee, you can safely stop spamming now and approach the music industry with some dignity! These tactics don't work, and if we can clean up our act, one at a time, we can change the public's perception of the independent artist from a nuisance to a valued, even critical part of the whole.

Here's a newsflash for the modern musician that few industry folks tell you.

Don't get stuck in the "everything is free" mentality.

This is a distinct change from my view in the last book. As much as musicians worldwide got caught up in the search for free ways to promote their music, I, too, got caught up in researching these methods. Don't get me wrong. There are many free ways to promote your music. Many of them are extremely effective. However, as more and more artists have sought out these methods, the balance has shifted and the paid methods have gone by the wayside.

The abundance of music blogs, podcasts, music distribution websites, licensing companies, music marketing books, industry gurus and online publications have given independent artists a convenient illusion; that you can become a buzz band while sitting in front of your computer. Just record a demo and you're ready to be the next Nirvana. The idea of actually working hard and saving money to put towards your music in the form of advertising, music video promotion, album promotion, radio promotion, and tour booking is a foreign idea to most musicians, even when the necessity seems so obvious.

Over the last few years I have seen both sides of the music industry, and I've learned quite a bit. One thing I've seen constantly is the extremely high expectations many artists have after posting their new album online. With no preparation or foresight put into their album release, they plan to impress Pitchfork, Stereogum and Rolling Stone with their chops. They look up online lists of the "Top 10 ways to promote your band for free" and think they're the first ones to try these methods. The problem with perspective here is that, somewhere along the line, we have separated the idea of starting a band from the process of starting a business.

Make no mistake. Unless you play music solely as a hobby, in which case you bought the wrong book, you must treat your band as a business.

As long as we have a monetary system, or trade goods in some shape or form, there will be business. Business itself is somewhat neutral. It's all about the ethics you bring to it and your responsibility to others as an honest human being.

If your band is a business, than what does that imply? All I can share with you are the things that lifted the wool from my own eyes, and hope that it's useful to you. In my own experience, I've seen friends and family open businesses, and each one required investment and great effort. A fashion-related business, for example, needed $30,000 to get off the ground running in order to order product, build a website, and pay for patents, shipping, and advertising. Dozens of hours needed to be put in to secure press as well. A moving and storage business required over $100,000 to pay for its storage containers, shipping, advertising, truck and employees.

Why is it, then, that independent musicians don't want to spend any money on promoting themselves? Record labels spend thousands of dollars breaking artists. To say simply that "you are broke" is just a defense mechanism. You can't say that to the tax man or to the energy company. So why do you say this to the music video director, the CD designer, the promotion company, or the tour booker? Of course, you must intuitively choose where you allot your funds. But it's important to know that if you spend a year writing and recording a brilliant album, and you don't bother to put any financial or serious promotional push behind it, you're effectively throwing it in the garbage. The artists who really treat their music as a business tend to make it further than the artists who don't.

This is where the issue of perception comes up again. Many artists fall into the trap of seeing business-savvy bands as sell-outs. We've all seen hordes of Nickelback wannabe bands playing at the local pub, and it's a sad sight. But this perception is limited. Trent Reznor is a great artist and businessman. So is Maynard James Keenan of Tool.

It's time to make some serious changes to our approach, to advance and empower ourselves. Let's get our music to the frontlines with honest practises and ignore the dinosaur-like mentality that dominates the industry.

The whole idea of this book is to give you as many helpful tools as possible to work with in the promotion of your music. There will be a good deal that you can use immediately. No need to read the book front to back. Work on it one tactic at a time if you like. The format of the book will all revolve around actual advice you can use.

Another few points to make: this book will focus mainly on online promotion of your music. Why? Well, for one, advice on booking tours, getting a manager, and making your way through the music business can be found in other fine books such as "Confessions of a Record Producer" by Moses Avalon. Secondly, this is what I know, and I'd rather share my expertise than venture into other areas like tour booking where I don't have experience. And plus, it all starts online. You need to build the foundation online, and why not make it a strong one?

Let's try to also keep our expectations reasonable. What you get out of the tools described in this book will depend strongly on how you use them. You may find that some promotional tactics work better for you than others. Expect your hard work to advance you and gain new fans, more hits to your website, more downloads of your music, and more press coverage. These things taken far enough will give you a strong reputation and poise you for bigger successes. But don't expect it to be linear according to your demands. Sometimes a review will seemingly have no impact at all on exposure, fan base or sales, but it's a matter of perspective. Have patience and let it cumulate. Every step forward, no matter how small, is a step in the right direction.

Some bands have gotten signed from online promotion and viral tactics alone, while some don't want to bother going near a computer. Unless your uncle is the CEO of EMI, or your band is making it to the top of the Los Angeles club circuit, you will need some serious online promotion on your side. It's all up to you and how hard you want to work at it.

We're going to try some methods not commonly used by today's breed of independent artists, such as Viral marketing, Guerrilla marketing and Behind-the-scenes marketing.

"It's all in the music, man. It's all in the meat."

– Kurt Cobain

TYPES OF MARKETING

Guerrilla Marketing:

According to Wikipedia, "Guerrilla marketing is an unconventional system of promotions that relies on time, energy and imagination rather than a big marketing budget. Typically, guerrilla marketing tactics are unexpected and unconventional; consumers are targeted in unexpected places, which can make the idea that's being marketed memorable, generate buzz, and even spread virally."

This is ideal and it's also one of our main goals. Get creative with all the ideas and tactics described in this book. Talk to people individually. Different tactics will work for different publications and individuals.

Independent musicians must be relentless and innovative with their marketing in order to achieve any level of success. Don't be afraid of doing things differently, so long as it works. There is no one rule, only what works.

Remember the examples rule: What works for a metal band may not work for a classical violinist. Each musician has their own niche, multiple niches in fact to exploit and use to their advantage. Chances are if you try to follow exactly what works for another band, it won't work. You need something that is your own or people will sense it and see through you. If it's not your own, then you have no business marketing it. If your biggest influence is Britney Spears, if you look like her, dress like her, and sound like her, then you are simply another copycat polluting the music world. The individual approach is essential for there to be any chance of deserved success. In an industry rife with imitation, those who let go of their programming and follow their hearts will naturally stand out.

Much of Guerilla marketing is about capturing attention with your tactic – doing things radically differently from the mainstream, and potentially your competitors as well.

[11]

And keep in mind Guerilla marketing has nothing to do with spamming, which will hurt more than help. Guerilla marketing means aggressively reaching out to and covering your potential markets while leaving no stone unturned. Be thorough and believe in your work. Make sure your tentacles reach everywhere necessary!

Keep in mind that although books have been written about Guerilla marketing in the past, it is not a set, rigid thing. Guerilla marketing is absolutely as original and cutting edge as you can imagine. It's only as creative as you are, so it may be time to channel your inner Sacha Baron Cohen and bring some attention to your music.

Sound good? Ok, now for the next tactic.

Behind-the-Scenes Marketing:

Behind-the-Scenes marketing is the tactic of manoeuvring behind the scenes to create a positive or powerful image for the buying public. Too many artists talk about themselves, whether it be on their Facebook walls or on countless message boards. It's very rare that people care, unfortunately, because a real connection hasn't been made.

The key to behind-the-scenes marketing is to get a high amount of other people talking about you rather than you talking about yourself.

UK pop/rock act Django Django made a major splash with their self-titled album. Do you think it was because of them entering contests and constantly posting on their social networks for their friends and fans to vote for them? Or perhaps sending out thousands of online invites to their shows? No. They generated a real, online buzz, as it was the bloggers, the radio hosts, the magazines, the podcasters, and then in turn the fans couldn't stop talking about them. They went viral.

For example, and we will discuss this in further detail later, contacting and befriending an individual writer at a music magazine and convincing him to review your band. Sure, HE knows that you looked him up and that you are an independent band desperately in need of coverage, but all the public sees is a good review on the next big thing. And the more you do this, the bigger and better you look. This will become one of the most important parts of your strategy to create a "frontline" image for your band.

Essentially, Behind-the-Scenes marketing is a term I use to describe a shift from the very embarrassing state of the independent music industry that currently has indie bands talking about themselves all the time. They beg their fans to vote for them. They post on the Twitter and Facebook pages of prospective companies instead of contacting them properly, in the process making their pleas for coverage very public. They harass bloggers by posting their audio and video links in the comments sections of blogs that have nothing to do with music submissions, once again, making their amateur approach public.

In my view, bands should let other people talk about them and the way to achieve this is by putting in real work behind the scenes. Plant thousands of seeds. Get in touch with as many writers as possible with an undeniably amazing product. Invite writers to your shows. Provide premieres and giveaways to music blogs. Make sure everyone familiar with your genre hears your music. Once the trendsetting mouths start talking, others listen and become inspired to speak. The music media is very much like the telephone game most of us played as children.

Behind-the-Scenes marketing is all about making connections from nothing, making those connections work for you by being personal, and using the results to leverage yourself and gain new successes.

That's the way it should be, right?

Viral Marketing:

What is viral marketing? According to Wikipedia, viral marketing refers to marketing techniques that use social networks to produce increases in brand awareness or to achieve other marketing objectives. It compares viral marketing to the spread of a computer virus.

The main idea is that, as a strategy, simply marketing with generic advertisements (*"You need this"* style of marketing) is on the extreme downswing, and is barely working in some markets.

Viral marketing is all about getting people to sell and advertise for you: Get your product talked about in the social networks, websites, forums, and blogs - and watch the magic happen. You no longer have anything to do with it. We'll go over a host of viral ideas in another chapter.

THE STARTING POINT

Record Your Music Properly:

Remember when we said that we want to keep this book potent and advice-based? As mundane as it sounds, we need to go over this point. If your music is not professional quality yet, THIS IS THE FIRST STEP! Make sure you prepare your best tracks and record a professional CD or series of tracks to promote yourself with. It's an obvious point – but the music must be intact. Don't rush the process in order to get online faster. Pay the money and get it recorded right.

I recently had a conversation with a musician friend who told me "I've tried listening to artists on Reverbnation, as if I was listening to a radio or podcast playlist, and I just couldn't get through it." The reason for this is that many artists are not using clear judgement, and they are hoping to present their work to the world too soon. This lowers both standards and expectations, and independent music gets more difficult to promote the more it becomes downgraded.

The market is already flooded with bands that have extremely high quality production. Being at their level is only the starting point, and it's the bare minimum you need to succeed in the music business. You may be able to score a great deal by recording in a home studio or with a music production student. The main thing is to have strong material that is recorded well. Not necessarily Michael Jackson quality of course, but it must be impressive!

There's nothing worse than going to a band's website and hearing garage or ghetto blaster quality recordings. It's a waste of everyone's time. If this sounds like your band, take your mp3's down until you re-record. Then you will be ready to start promoting. Even if you get three songs properly recorded, it's better than a full album of ghetto blaster noise. No one in the

[15]

industry expects a fifteen song album these days. Some bands choose to release an mp3 per month, or a four song digital EP release. All the rules have been broken, so do what's right for *your* band.

If you are financially unprepared to record even one song professionally, you will need to either fundraise socially (through Kickstarter.com or other methods) or get a second job and make it happen. How will you do anything else if you can't do this? You should not be listed ANYWHERE on the internet with unprofessional content representing you – even on local websites and forums. If everyone followed this advice, independent music websites would be more popular, and much more rewarding to scour through.

Imagine our social networks without the amateur garbage?

This point is not to complain. Each one of us is responsible for cleaning up our own act, and watching closely what we bring to the world through our thoughts, words, and other contributions. The more we utilize patience, innovation, and accountability, the better.

Get Content:

What do we mean by content? Well, you have your CD or EP recorded and you want to get started with online promotion. You will need at least a biography, some quality artwork, and some professionally done photos. Don't be one of those unknown artists promoting their new "single" to the world! Have an impressive, professional body of work from the very start.

Biography:

Many independent artists struggle with biographies, and it's no wonder. For many artists, they know that they haven't "done anything" yet, so they feel the best option is to over-compensate. This is not the case. Think of reading a biography as an equivalent experience to meeting someone. The best tactic is to keep it concise and information-based, to impress with the facts and not the over-hyped propaganda.

One thing I have noticed, as a consistent pattern in the thousands of artist biographies I have read, is the tendency to over-emphasize your story. You need to have the ability to step outside yourself and put yourself in the shoes of the reader, whether they are an industry person or a prospective fan. How much about you would they possibly want to read?

Far too many biographies start with something like "David Smith has had a love for all things music since the age of three, when he began to teach himself singing, guitar, and drums." They usually go on with tales of junior high bands and an impressive number of instruments played, including clarinet, saxophone, and recorder. Two pages later, the bio is done and you have to wonder if they contemplated the process at all. While David's music may very well have been amazing, the reader would most likely abandon ship before listening. It's important to be able to spot what will come across as arrogant.

It takes a discerning eye to be able to choose what is relevant to share, and what no one is going to care about. Your family and friends can't help in this regard, because in most cases they won't be honest with you. For this reason, hiring a professional bio writer, or someone outside the band, is also a great option. You are often too close to yourself to talk about yourself.

Another good rule of thumb is to keep it short, and without language such as "The Evil Lizards are the best band to come out of North America since Metallica." As great as this statement sounds, it will just end up making you look like jerks.

It will not have the desired effect (Metallica fans and media personnel foaming at the mouth to check out your music). As you gain press (which we'll get to) you can also add press quotes to your bio. Why? Because it's ok for OTHER PEOPLE to brag about you – but you can't do it yourself. Remember that!

It's also ok, even recommended, to talk about your influences in your band's biography. Until you are as big as U2, go ahead and mention who influenced your sound. As long as it's done in the correct way, it will definitely entice more people to give your music a chance, and also help your search engine results, successfully tying your band name to the influences of your choice. Just be sure to keep it humble and clear.

When in doubt, read Wikipedia. It seems counter-intuitive, but when I write biographies, I try to keep it concise and fact-based as if it was a Wikipedia page on the artist. When you read an artist's Wikipedia, you are not going to get a whole bunch of promotional language. You are going to get something stronger and much more convincing – cold, hard facts.

Proper comparisons example: "Inspired by the likes of Tool, Metallica, Queens of the Stone Age and Lamb of God, the Evil Lizards showcase their own aggressive brand of metal-infused rock music."

The reason a statement like this would work is because the band is mentioning very successful bands, as a tribute of sorts, while not making the language overly promotional. This quote is meant to entice fans of the aforementioned bands to wonder, "What do the Evil Lizards sound like? If they sound anything like a cross between Tool, Metallica and Queens of the Stone Age, they must be awesome!"

Wikipedia style example: "Sonic Youth is an American alternative rock band from New York City, formed in 1981. Their most recent lineup consisted of Thurston Moore (guitar and vocals), Kim Gordon (bass guitar, vocals, and guitar), Lee Ranaldo (guitar and vocals), Steve Shelley (drums), and Mark Ibold (guitar and bass)." (Taken from Sonic Youth's Wikipedia page)

Formatting your band's bio to look more like a Wikipedia article makes it look more official, and even though you may not think so, you will have many more bloggers and media personnel take the time to learn about you when you are not going on about yourself. Let the music do the talking.

Sample Band Biography:

Here's a sample band biography to help you. Remember, the bio is for the media, the music industry, future contacts, as well as your fans. It should read like a fact sheet, but keep it creative, energetic, and useful.

Be sure it represents your band.

Make them want to listen.

1st Paragraph: You will need an introduction. This should be a sentence that clearly defines you, your band name or alias, where you're from, your specific genre of music (eclectic brand of space rock, punk-infused speed metal – make it interesting but don't lie!), etc. You can also add a positive quote you have received from a website, blog, radio or magazine review. (Rock Magazine calls the Sonic Spacemen "A real rock juggernaut…the sound of the future".)

2nd Paragraph: This paragraph will go over the purpose of the bio. What is your band up to? If you have a new CD coming out, this should be the topic of the paragraph. Promotional information such as tours, events, or music videos to support the album should also be mentioned here. Keep it concise.

3rd and 4th Paragraphs: Relevant information on band members (edit out the bit about your drummer being the greatest player since Danny Carrey), band accomplishments (festival spots, awards, licensing deals, glowing reviews, etc), experience (tours, albums, song writing), and information about the forming of the band can be delved into here. Once again, it's critical that this area is concise.

Ending: Summarize current activities and events, the goals of the band, and be sure to include another raving press quote here.

Remember, you do not need an epic story to get noticed. Let the music speak for itself. The shorter you can make your bio, the better. You do not need four paragraphs. You just need to present yourself accurately and professionally, and do not get in the way of the music. I remember reviewing an artist who claimed that his album was "the best rock album since Dark Side of the Moon". Needless to say, my perception of him was clouded from there on.

I saw him as egotistical and out of touch, and there was no way his music could come close to the lofty heights his ego was reaching for. So how could I relate to his music?

Band Artwork:

The artwork you choose will represent your band, so make sure it's strong and consistent with your message and style. There are many independent and professional graphic designers who will create custom art to help you stand out from the crowd. If you are talented in the area of graphic design, do it yourself! If you want to learn, there are plenty of courses available, as well as online tutorials on graphic design. This is where having no rules can help you. For some artists, even hand drawn, or very low quality art, suits their image perfectly. Remember, music fans check out new bands in many cases because of interesting or intriguing artwork, whether it's a CD cover or a band logo.

Of course, many artists (and business owners) stretch themselves too thin by trying to do everything. It's NEVER a bad idea to hire a professional. After all, this is your image we are talking about. Why not scour through the countless local bands in your area and take note of the ones with eye-catching artwork. Usually, either the artist will be credited on their website, or the band will be happy to tell you who their artist is. Unless the band in question are doing very well or heavily touring, chances are the artist is doing their work "on the cheap". While cheap is not always best, if you find the right balance and work with good people, you can get a great looking album cover and booklet for under $1,000.

Other great ways to find a band artist are to post want ads in your local free classified websites, or how about hosting a fan art contest? In many cases, fan-driven contests produce some of the best art, because there are way more people capable of incredible art out there than those who earn money doing so. As in music, so it is in art! Giving credit and publicity to the artist as a reward for their hard work is often all that is required.

Many bands end up spending too much money on their album art. It is important to have the full picture in mind when you approach an album. Yes, it's ideal that you have an iconic album cover, but if you're leaving no funds to actually promote the album, it really doesn't add up. It's just a great work of art on your CD shelf, or possibly 1,000 great works of art collecting dust in the garage. This is why it is important to budget and not pay more attention to one aspect of success than another.

Band Photos:

For photos, there should be plenty of amateur, yet professional and ambitious photographers in your area who are looking to photograph bands and are happy to provide you with the high quality photos in return for credit (Photo taken by___), or a small fee. Sometimes student photographers will take pictures of bands free, simply for experience or word-of-mouth promotion. With the improvement of quality of digital cameras, photos can also be done yourself or by someone in your circle of friends. Even iPhones and Android Smartphones have such advanced built-in cameras that they both take great shots – just make sure the photographer knows what they are doing. Try to do something eye catching and original with your band promo shots, but keep it professional.

Remember, these will represent you on your website, and also be used in the media when you are interviewed, reported on or reviewed. Taking photos on your cell phone or cheap camera is not going to cut it. Hire someone who is serious about photography and trying to build their portfolio (hint: they will give you a deal.)

Another important tip about getting photos for your band – Take it seriously and dress appropriately. This doesn't necessarily mean you need to wear a suit. You must make it suit your music though. Consider the band photos you see from the millions of bands flooding the market today. Jeans and t-shirts, right? It's up to you, but the "show up in your street clothes" approach just doesn't seem like an eye-catching option anymore in today's option-overloaded marketplace.

The band's that will stand out in the new marketplace are the ones who have an image. The ones who are daring enough to be different will succeed. Whether this means that your band dresses up in army fatigues, Alice in Wonderland costumes, crimson robes, suits, tribal attire, masks, or zombie makeup, you have got to do something to stand out in the crowd.

Think about it this way. How would you dress to your sister's wedding? How would you dress if you were to have a meeting with your idol? How about if you were to perform a work of art that is very dear to you?

If music is unimportant to you – stop! If it IS important to you, discard your subconscious negativities and give it the respect it deserves. Dress appropriately. Now this may be an extreme example, but I was perusing a local music magazine this morning. It seemed every independent band I came across were posing in alleys, lying in a field, trying on animal masks, or pushing each other around in a shopping cart with big smiles on their faces. Guess how many of these bands intrigued me?

I assumed right away that their music was subpar and lazy, just like their image. Then I came across a feature article on the metal band Behemoth. Even if I did not listen to metal, I would admit it's an extremely effective image, and I might just listen to their music out of curiosity.

Ok, now that you have your music professionally recorded and you've got some slick looking content, you're ready to build a web site.

BUILDING A WEBSITE

Here is another obvious one. Yes, you can start with a simple Facebook page, and start the website later (just try not to let this go on for long). You WILL need your own domain (such as www.bestbandever.com) before you decide to release your CD. This is for a few reasons: It makes you look more professional. If you use it properly, the official website will push you ahead of the "social media horde." Having your own website allows you to be taken more seriously, and shows the industry that you have your "ducks in a row."

It gives your band a more 'permanent' image than a band with only social media. Having a strong website really demonstrates commitment and potential staying power. It shows that your intention is to last a long time.

It's a home base to market your product (your CD's and merchandise) and customize your e-store. It's your home base, free of outside voices (except the ones YOU approve). Give people something exciting and a reason to visit again.

Better Sound Quality Options:
People may check you out on long-forgotten but still popular directories, such as MySpace for a preview of your sound. But MySpace sound quality is quite poor. It's notoriously poor, in fact. An official website will give you options for higher quality previews of your music.

Mailing List Capability and membership options, E-team registration, free downloads and other promotion, design and marketing options: Get people involved in your official website. Make it a destination place for people to frequent online. Create incentives to encourage people to sign up for your website, e-team or mailing list. We'll expand on this later.

How do you build a website?

Well, the good news is you don't really need to know how to build a website – or at least not by any html method.

First you'll want to buy your domain at a hosting website such as www.godaddy.com. There are many reasons why to stick with a .com or a .net address. Some people may be unsure about whether to visit your website or not if it has a strange or unknown address. It's simply easier for people to find you and it's the most trustworthy and recognizable way to do it.

So if your ideal address www.evillizards.com is taken, try
www.evillizards.net,
www.evillizardsband.com,
www.evillizardsmusic.com.
Make sure it is easy to remember, and makes sense for you.

Next, you can get a cheap hosting account at sites such as www.hostgator.com and then build your site from there. If you are familiar with html, you'll be ready to customize your official website with no trouble.

If you're unfamiliar with doing it yourself, you can achieve just about everything you'll require by setting your domain up with Wordpress.com software (hint: you can do this automatically by choosing this option on Hostgator.com) and buying a quality template from a site such as themeforest.net, a directory of attractive web templates for just about every need.

While Wordpress can be frustrating at times, it is very simple to use overall, especially if you educate yourself and simply google the answer whenever you have a question. I have found Wordpress to be a great solution for my own website www.independentmusicpromotions.com.

For an in-depth tutorial on how to set up a Wordpress website for a band, visit my friend Joshua Smotherman's very informative article on the topic at Middle Tennessee Music.

http://www.midtnmusic.com/how-to-install-self-hosted-wordpress-to-manage-your-bands-website/.

Another option is to hire a professional web designer. If you've got original ideas for your website and want to stand out from the crowd, this could be the way to go. Just don't get too ambitious. Remember, your website will be like your press package. You don't need all the bells and whistles, just the necessities.

Do Not Spend Too Much On Web Design:

The days of spending $1,000 or more on custom websites are long gone. There are MUCH better ways that you can spend $1,000 on your music career than getting a website done.

For every web designer who offers to charge you $1,000 for a quality website there will be ten who offer you $250. Shop around and do not hesitate to hire an ambitious student. Students need the extra cash and can do a great job. Also, make sure that the web designer knows how to create a mailing list template (or insert a pre-existing one for you), and design a website according to the marketing criteria that you will require as an independent musician trying to advance yourself.

If you want to build the site yourself and be in control of everything – I don't blame you. And the good news is that you can certainly do it.

Two popular ways to do this are specifically aimed at independent artists. Both options are reputable and roughly the same price. Both offer custom website designs that bands and artists can individualize with their own art and photos. They both also offer high storage space for music and media. Mailing lists, e-store capability, blogs, and forums are other features both sites offer. You will definitely need these features to effectively promote your band online.

If you decide to go this route, check out the links below and decide for yourself. I have had good experiences with both companies, but Bandzoogle would get my recommendation for a superior administration, better template options and many more extensive features offered, especially for the inexperienced webmaster: www.bandzoogle.com, www.hostbaby.com

A fresh, new service brought to my attention is an innovative company called One Sheet, which you can find at www.onesheet.com. This seems to be an excellent option for independent artists, as it takes all of your social profiles and the information/updates within them, and organizes them into a central website, or one-sheet. Content that you upload to YouTube, Facebook, CDBaby, Amazon, Twitter, and a host of others gets posted here.

This is where the industry is headed, because people simply have less time now—especially people working in the music industry. They want easy access to your material, so why not have it all in one place?

What Should You Put On Your Website?

Well, you can get creative, but there are some things that your website must have. Here, I'll go over a popular, tried-and-true method of building a sales-based site, but for full disclosure I should tell you that I have a new favorite "free" method, which I'll also go over. First, the sales method and the big three required for its execution:

The main page: The first thing visitors to your site will typically see. Do not set up a splash or intro page! This will drive away more people than it will entice. Your main page should include a brief introduction so people know what site they are on. It can have a news section. It's also a good idea to have a sidebar with option to sign up for your mailing list or e-team.

The music page: Post your music on this page (obviously). Don't be a prude with the sound samples and previews. 30-second previews are a thing of the past and they will make you look like a chump. Be generous. Offer a few free downloads or a bunch. Give people something to take with them and spread virally. Brief information on the album and a few press clippings can be on this page too provided they don't take too much space.

Buy the CD, or Checkout page: This is the most important page of your website. You do want to sell, don't you? Your whole website should be based around getting people from the main page to the music page and then to your e-store page. There are other necessary elements of a band's website but these are the three most important. The other categories can even be subsections (accessible by drop-down menus) of these three.

The Other Pieces of the Puzzle

The Bio: Let people know your band story. Make it available to the press and the fans. Keep it concise and engaging.

Contact: People need to know how to get a hold of you. Make it clear and easy. Include your email and phone number. You don't want to miss any opportunities from companies or questions from fans.

Photos: Post your professional press photos and live photos here. Make sure they're good ones and don't post too many. 10 great shots work much better than 200 live shots taken by your deadbeat uncle. Keep it clean and slick looking!

Mailing list: Put this on your main page, and ideally every page on your website. This will continually remind people that there is a way to keep up to date with all the happenings of your band. This can be as important as a CD sale. Let your network grow.

Blog: Blog away on Wordpress or Blogger. What's your story? What are your opinions? Are you funny? Want to write some music reviews of your own? (This is a great way to use relevant keywords and attract new visitors to your website.)

Why not post song lyrics or unreleased material? Make it interesting and engaging. Make people want to come back and check out what you are going to say next. It's also important to spread your blog posts around with the use of keywords and RSS feeds. If the music blogs don't cover you, why not covertly start your own blog?

Press: This is where you post your extensive list of press quotes and accolades. You'll want to do this with permission from the media in question of course. Post links to every piece of press you get. Also, be sure to post interviews with the band. Keep this page full of content. Make it impressive. This will be no trouble once you start reaching out to the media in the right way.

Links: There are different opinions on whether to have a links section or not, and it's really up to you. It is a good thing to have if you want something to barter with when approaching websites for press coverage, so I'll include the information.

Offering banner exchanges or a link exchange is a great form of cross-promotion. Link exchanges with other bands can get you more fans. Basically, at the independent level you will want to get on as many websites as possible, and link exchanges can be a good way to do it. Want a good place to start? Try the Indie Bible link exchange at http://www.indiebible.com/ile/index.shtml

Just make sure to allot your time accordingly, and don't let link exchanges take all your energy. Choose sites in your niche and measure your results.

The only trouble with links sections is the professionalism. Having too many large banners can make an artist page look unprofessional. So can off-topic and low quality websites. Many artists decide to forego the links section altogether, and this is a valid option I would tend to choose myself.

Selling as the focus of your website: The two main points to launching your music website with a sales design are to spread your music across the globe, and to sell.

That is exactly why the information you provide about yourself should be clean and somewhat minimal, while the focus of the website should be on your products (your CD and merchandise).

When you buy a custom t-shirt on EBay, do you care who made it? Do you want to know the company biography? Probably not. You have to present your CD as a product, because this is what people will want to buy. You'll simply cause confusion if you make yourself the main attraction and keep your store hidden away. People can't rent you out. They are buying something you have created.

Don't worry! This is not to say that no one is going to check out your photos or your biography page. You will certainly have fans who are interested in knowing every little thing about you. We're just saying that the best way to set up your website is to focus on selling your products. How are they going to get to your products if your website is overly jammed up with too many photos of you, a guestbook filled with comments from your family, and a 3-page biography covering everything since the first jam?

Sometimes more is less, and extra content can actually work against you, making you look amateur and unprofessional. It's much better to create a mystique than to reveal yourself as a desperate, starving artist – even if that's what you are. No one needs to know. Get out of the way and let them get the products!

Give them a straight path!

The Backwards Method to Music Success

The music industry has changed so much in the past 10 years, that there has emerged a "free path", or, a backwards method of promoting, and this presents another way to go when approaching your website design. I present this as another option, as many people are tired of the "information overload" so common on the internet. When you provide something simply and directly, it can pay off, and people spread the word accordingly. Please note that this "backwards method" is my suggested method. While the sales tactic previously described works for many bands, I have seen many more forward-thinking artists make huge strides by making their music free and easily accessible.

The reason I call it the "backwards method" is because it requires both patience and foresight. Most artists are expecting too much, as far as sales, and this method demolishes that idea by advocating exposure first, sales later.

Canadian R & B sensation The Weeknd (http://the-weeknd.com) broke many of the traditional rules of the music industry, as well as the illusions of how independent artists should promote themselves when he released 3 high quality albums online within a year's time. His website was simple. There was no bio. No photos. Nothing. Just a big photo of the album cover in question and a button that said "Download", as well as an email contact to make sure he could be reached by the industry. If you wanted more information, the social network buttons were available on the side, neatly out of the way.

With no frills, no gimmicks, and a high amount of stunningly good content, this built trust and aggressive word-of-mouth. With no email even required to download the album, this allowed new fans to rapidly recommend the artist, as they knew none of their friends would be hassled with any mailing list or email notifications. This is a fairly new method, and it requires the same amount of hard work as traditional methods because, after all, people still need to find your website.

Many artists don't yet understand this method. They ask "Well, how am I going to make money then?" That's typically the main concern. My answer is "Why don't you build your name first so you can then make money?" Thinking you're going to make money on a completely unknown band is insane, and that harmful illusion needs to go. It causes many artists to become paralyzed and unable to see beyond the amount of 99 cent downloads they're raking in (which in most cases is only a few). People like free stuff. It's as simple as that. This makes free digital releases a wonderful option for independent bands who want to build their fan-bases quickly and organically.

As opposed to devaluing the product (as it clearly didn't in The Weeknd's case), if done correctly, it can show an immense confidence in your work and its ability to spread, creating its own momentum. Independent artists have no idea how many people turn away from a band when they can't find a free download of their album. It's neither good nor bad. It's the way things are. The utility of these people is sometimes greatly underestimated. When someone "steals" your album, it doesn't necessarily end there. They may post your video on their blog or their Facebook wall. They may give the album to their friends. They may put you on their online playlists for Google's bots to pick up on. This all feeds in to your hype. You can shut it down because you imagine getting 99 cents a song, but this suggestion is just a nudge to hopefully show a bigger picture.

[30]

When your music is out in the world being spread as opposed to being hoarded, you are far more likely to generate strong word-of-mouth, which can attract licensing deals, festival offers, and label attention. That said, your music needs to be unbelievable and you must put time and effort in for this to work. Whether you choose the selling method, the free method, or a combination of both, you need to have your music online and easily accessible.

GET YOUR MUSIC ONLINE

Now that you have your website up with your samples, you will want people to discover you and your music. There are quite a few ways to do this. Besides your official website, one of the most obvious things to do is to sign up for popular social networks such as Facebook and Twitter (if you haven't done so already). Also, it's wise to set yourself up on Bandcamp.com, Soundcloud.com, Last.fm and Reverbnation.com to name a few.

Many argue over what are the best places to share your music. My suggestion is to put it everywhere and keep tabs on the lot through a service such as www.onesheet.com. They're all just tools that will be effective or ineffective according to how hard you work. A resume only gets seen when you send it out and follow up. It also has to be impressive for you to get the job.

Facebook.com

Facebook is probably the most misunderstood promotional tool used by independent musicians today. It's the largest marketing opportunity available for musicians, and can be lucratively effective when used properly.

The most difficult thing for musicians to understand in regards to Facebook is the low amount of engagement from their fans. This issue is typically due to a lack of understanding of something called Edgerank. Edgerank is the algorithm that Facebook uses in order to decide how often your content shows up on your fan's news feeds. Its activity is not biased. It's based on participation. That's why it's so critical for people to like and share your posts as much as possible. If your post doesn't show up in someone's news feed, there's very little chance they'll get the message.

To explain it simply, Edgerank attempts to predict what every Facebook user wants to see in their news feed. Hundreds, sometimes thousands of friends, companies, and pages are always competing for space on the Facebook news feed, as this is valuable real estate.

Fan engagement guides the whole process. The more people "like", share, or comment on your posts, the more they will see your news come up in the future. On top of this, activity on a post virtually guarantees that it will be seen by more outsiders and new potential fans. Start with friends, family, and your core fan base. Let them know how important it is that they support your posts. Things should organically grow exponentially from there as distribution inevitably improves. Don't let your posts sink like stones.

More information on Edgerank can be found here: http://www.insidefacebook.com/2011/12/27/edgerank-and-graph-rank-defined.

It's also critical to really engage with fans on Facebook. Don't just promote your content. **Ask questions** to ensure comments and debate. Like their comments and always respond.

Use photos in your posts as much as possible, and not always ones that have to do with your music. Something eye-catching or funny could get attention. Think of what grabs your eye when logging into your own Facebook account. There's no reason why your band's account can't post amazing content that could either make someone's day or at least get them commenting. Align it with your life philosophy.

Facebook also offers other tools such as Geo-targeting, which allows you to direct a post only towards a particular location. This can be very useful, especially if you're writing to your hometown fans or reaching out to a city you'll be hitting on your current tour.

As far as setting up the ultimate Facebook page, quality content is the main thing. Many bands make the mistake of posting a sarcastic statement that they think is humorous in their description section. To save you some time, this is rarely impressive. Be sure to fill out every section properly, and include your full, professional biography on your Facebook page. Include your email and phone contacts. People in the music industry check out artists via their Facebook pages all the time, so the information must be ready for them as well as potential fans.

Facebook gives you the opportunity to choose a series of featured likes, so why not build some alliances with other bands you believe in and cross-promote that way? Those who trust your opinion will check out your favorite links, and vice versa, so this can be influential.

Use **Facebook events** to promote all your live events, and it's always a good idea to set up pages well in advance (a separate event page for each tour date). The more live dates, the better, as your event pages get spread more and more. Encourage fans in each area to spread the links and create incentives.

Exclusive content also does very well on Facebook, and those who treat their Facebook fans like a special club often generate more rabid support. How about posting an HD live performance just for your Facebook fans, and anyone who reposts gets free admission to your next show, or perhaps an unreleased track delivered to their inbox?

Another way many artists have gained popularity on Facebook is by encouraging fans and friends to take photos at their live performances and tag the band later. Want to try this from a different angle? Take a bunch of photos at each of your shows and have people tag themselves. This can help you reach a ton of new listeners, as everyone loves to see himself or herself in a picture. In fact, this could end up being one of your most powerful promotion tools.

Facebook Ads are encouraged as an organic way to grow your fan base. They can be targeted to any demographic, location, or series of keywords, and can work with any budget. If you have $2 a day, you can still run a campaign. Make sure you use your best promo shot, preferably one clearly showing your face. The headline can contain a short press quote or a relevant comparison to a popular band. Choose something that you would click on to discover a new band. Many bands experiment, and when they find something that works, they not only do it consistently, but they up their budget to gain more new fans. You would be surprised what consistent advertising and proper use of keywords can do for your band. You may find yourself gaining so many new fans that you raise your budgets accordingly!

Re-post other people's content that you feel your audience would enjoy. Has a friend's band released a new video? Is there an interesting Smashing Pumpkins article on Stereogum? A website who has supported you in the past just posted a new blog? People notice when you re-post their content. In most cases, they'll support you in return. It's about consistently nurturing relationships. On top of this, artists should be commenting on other relevant Facebook pages and encouraging that back-and-forth, as well as creating more visibility for themselves. If you're not reaching out to every good band, radio show, podcast, blog, company and magazine relevant to your band, you're missing out on valuable visibility.

Facebook offers a series of widgets and "like" boxes that can be embedded into your official website or blog. These can be just as critical for gaining new fans as your promotions within Facebook.

Looking for a snazzy design for your Facebook page, now that you know the ins and outs? Many companies offer this, and a simple Google search will lead you in the right direction. Band Spaces (www.bandspaces.com) offer a variety of Facebook design services for those looking to spruce things up.

Also, Wildfire, the number one application for sweepstakes and contests, is fully integrated with Facebook and designed to help bands go viral. When someone enters your sweepstakes, it appears on their Facebook wall, showing up in the news feeds of their friends. Bands who use Wildfire can find their popularity snowballing fast. If you hold a sweepstakes, make sure the prize has some cash or a gift card along with your band swag. This will allow you to sneak your contest into multiple categories on the popular sweepstakes websites and get thousands more entries. More information is on Wildfire at www.wildfireapp.com.

Twitter:

Much like Facebook, Twitter is meant to be used to build relationships, and communicate your message in a poignant way. The most popular accounts are the ones people gather around to hear the scoop "straight from the horse's mouth" as the saying goes. The most important rule to using Twitter is to post about things you actually care about. It should be a reflection of you.

Many bands use Twitter to post their updates for months, wondering why there's no interaction on their profile. Replies could be a key ingredient and necessity here. Not only should you reply to your fans when they tag you in a post, but its good practise to reply to other relevant posts as well. Replies are public, so keep that in mind. This works to your benefit as far as visibility for your band goes. Replies spike your engagement rate and also let your fans know you're a real person. No one wants to talk to an automatic tweet.

Tagging (@) and then the account name) others on Twitter is another very important part of your promotion plan. Do this to give someone your thumbs up or a thank you, or to recommend them to your fans. If a publication does a piece on you, you'll want to tag them to say thanks. Just discovered an amazing new artist? Tag them. Pay it forward and see what happens.

Twitter also allows hashtags, which act as labels or keywords in order to arrange tweets by topic. Use only one at a time. For example, if your post was regarding Coachella, your hashtag would be #Coachella. Hashtags are used for events and news stories, and can be a great way to either start or join a conversation.

When you hover over a tweet, you will have an option to "retweet" it. The **retweet** function is invaluable, as it's a way of showing someone you respect what they're saying, or you found their post useful. It's a display of support, and can also be a great way for you to provide content to your followers. Note: others retweeting your posts can be lucrative.

Twitter also offers comprehensive advertising options that are similar to Facebook in that they are customizable and able to target any demographic. If you're new to Twitter, why not focus on your local area to generate a strong fan base? You can either promote specific tweets or your account as a whole. It's worthwhile to look into both, but keep in mind that Twitter can be an intensely self-interested bunch, with most users following you only so you'll follow them back. Enticing tweets pointing to your new, free album release may be a better option to go with provided it's targeted effectively.

Last.fm:

Last.fm is essentially a powerful music discovery tool that combines social networking and online radio. An industry friend recently told me that many bands neglect Last.fm, but it acts as an accurate statement showing where an artist is at any given moment in time, perhaps more than any other social network. After all, Facebook and Twitter are easily manipulated through the purchase of fans. Providing full information and promoting your Last.fm profile is a must.

One of Last.fm's best features is its similar bands feature, which helps people discover new music, both through the website and online radio. When signing up, it's best to choose cult favourites – small to mid-level bands as opposed to too many major acts like Tool or Nine Inch Nails. This will allow you to show up higher in the similar artists search function rather than be buried by hundreds of other groups.

Make your songs freely available and downloadable if you want your music to spread fast. Tag them properly so they come up when someone searches "Swedish death metal" for example. Similar to other social networks, Last.fm enables you to befriend others and comment on their profiles. The same rules apply. Keep it genuine and engaging. Like Soundcloud, Last.fm also has advanced group features that can lead to added exposure in your genre.

Bandcamp.com:

Bandcamp has a very clean layout, and because of this it has become the undisputed preference of music bloggers. They will often visit the artist's Bandcamp page in place of the official website. The genius of Bandcamp is that they have left no room for rambling, advertisements, spam, or useless content. It allows the artist to store high quality artwork and music, as well as providing convenient song and album widgets that any blogger can easily post on their websites. There are endless promotion features available for Bandcamp albums. Social media "like" buttons on individual tracks and albums, as well as Twitter sharing options are easily accessible. Downloads from Bandcamp can be in any chosen format, and this is another positive. Another great feature is the pricing system they offer, which includes both free and the very popular "pay what you want" model made famous by artists like Radiohead and Nine Inch Nails.

If you choose to go the free route via Bandcamp, you will find that there are many music bloggers and writers who are there to support you. Simply google "Free Bandcamp albums," or check out the vast free music resources such as the Free Music Archive and submit your album for consideration. The Bandcamp music player is fast and convenient, making the experience of checking out an artist a good one.

Soundcloud:

When artists like Lil Wayne and Kanye West release new music, they typically do so on Soundcloud, and that alone should tell you something. Soundcloud.com is a stunningly good music community, and it, too, is a favorite amongst music bloggers. Soundcloud provides many of the simple features that Bandcamp does, while also serving as a community for both musicians and the media who support them. There are endless groups, publications, podcasts and radio shows listed on Soundcloud, and they all have dropboxes where artists can submit their music for consideration. Although I have found Soundcloud's search function to be very poor, I am sure they will make improvements as they go along, and it's still well worth spending some time searching for opportunities within your genre on the site.

Soundcloud also distributes music using widgets and apps, thus allowing the music to go viral. Allowing files to be easily embedded just about anywhere has put Soundcloud ahead of the pack. And what's more? It can be combined with Twitter and Facebook too so that your fans can hear your new creations right away without any re-posting on your part. Have a work-in-progress that isn't quite ready for public sharing? Not to worry. Soundcloud has an option for private links as well.

Soundcloud also features a host of useful apps such as Root Music, which can be found at http://soundcloud.com/apps/root music: Root Music allows artists to customize their Facebook page while integrating their Soundcloud tracks. Flavors.me is another app that aggregates services in a similar way to One Sheet, organizing all your profiles in one central location. Check out the app at http://soundcloud.com/apps/flavors. Interested in a mobile app to promote your Soundcloud material to cell phone users? Check out Mobile Roadie at http://soundcloud.com/apps/ mobile-roadie.

Reverbnation:
Reverbnation.com is possibly the least important of the three, and some criticize it of becoming similar to a modern version of Myspace. Even though Reverbnation is flooded with bands, some music fans and industry people use it to look for new music. Reverbnation offers many services to independent artists, and I would encourage all artists to at least take a close look. They do charge for some of their services, and with these, it's important to research and possibly try them out, but if they turn out to be ineffective, your dollars could be better spent elsewhere. Some artists report that the ratios of success when submitting to

Reverbnation opportunities are higher than that of Sonicbids. They currently offer everything from licensing to music festivals.

As with anything else, approach them neutrally and test as you move. It's also important to think of them only as part of your web presence.

iTunes is another service you should have your music on. But hold on a minute. Signing up straight through iTunes can be sticky. They are fussy about their database and entries can take a long time to be accepted... but there IS a way around it and we suggest it wholeheartedly.

CDBaby:

CDBaby is a great service and one of the best ways for independent artists to start to sell product. They were built from the bottom up with independent artists in mind. The reason they are thriving is because their formula works.

Here's how CDBaby.com works:

1. You send CDBaby your CDs and they take care of the rest for you — they process the orders and ship the goods on your behalf. Just add links to CDBaby on your website to make them either your main payment option or a secondary option when people visit your online store.

To kick things off, fill out their submission form at

http://members.cdbaby.com/signup/

2. CDBaby.com will make a Web page specifically to showcase your CD on their Web site.

It includes sound clips, links back to your own Web site, reviews, and all of the text and descriptions you want. You fill in the details and decide what gets posted. Be sure to include lots of relevant keywords to attract new visitors to your CDBaby sales page. Also, this site is perfect for press quotes and contact information.

3. There is a one-time charge to set up a new CD in their store. It doesn't matter how many CD's you sell. They will not charge you any further fees or remove your CD from the database at any time.

4. CDBaby takes all credit card orders for your CD, online or through their toll-free phone number, and ships it to customers within hours. They e-mail you every time your CD is sold to tell you who bought it. "Break out the champagne" is the phrase.

They also provide the person's email address, which you should keep track of and add to your mailing list (important tip).

5. The CDBaby.com deal is non-exclusive. There are no contracts to sign. CDBaby.com is not a record label or a publisher. It's only a record store.

6. You don't need a UPC barcode to sell at CDBaby. Though if you do have one already, they will report your sales to SoundScan. You don't need to have your CDs shrink-wrapped.

You don't need to upload mp3 files or send them graphics or anything else. Just fill out their submission form at

http://members.cdbaby.com/signup/ and send them five CDs. They do the rest.

CRITICAL POINT: Remember we mentioned iTunes and how it's a difficult service to get into? If you sign up for CDBaby, just opt into their digital distribution program (also free) and you will automatically get listed in iTunes, as well as eMusic, Rhapsody, Amazon, Napster, PayPlay, Ruckus and a host of others.

In order to keep up with other digital distributors, CDBaby has recently expanded its services, opting to include more licensing and business opportunities for its artists. They have a podcast that features CDBaby artists and also a recommended album section.

So now you have your CD pressed (we're assuming this because you'll need your product for online promotion), your content (bio and photos) professionally done, and you've set up your website, Bandcamp, Soundcloud, Reverbnation and CDBaby accounts. Your music is also being showcased at the most popular digital services such as iTunes and Amazon.com.

So now you're on the verge, right? No. This is where most bands go completely wrong. They think that they will record an album, get some photos done, put up a website, and become big stars. The truth is, and this is true for any website or business, if you have a website but don't promote it, you don't have a website. If you have a product but don't advertise it, you have no product. You don't exist! So the most important thing to focus on is how to begin "existing" as a product in the public eye.

Let's look at the positive. You now have the groundwork laid out, and this is critical. You've created (part of) a professional image for yourself, made yourself available to the public, and made your product available. You have the "potential to exist", to put it humorously. Now you need to promote yourself! After this groundwork, now you're at the starting line!

Since the idea of this book is usefulness to the independent musician, we're going to go over a long list of practical ways to promote your music. Each tactic will have a description and some external links where necessary. Here we go. Let's jump in.

Search Engine Optimization:

People typically arrive at websites in three ways: through the use of search engines, clicking links from other websites, or simply by typing in the website address. Even though search engines alone will not complete your promotional arsenal, they will be important.

One thing to make sure of is that in the title tag of your webpage is the name of your band or the keywords you would like to be found with. The title tag is similar to the title of a book. It has to say who you are and get people interested as well. The title tag is used by almost every search engine that uses spiders to crawl your website, and as such, it is the most important tag on your website. The length of your title tag should be a maximum of 70 characters long and this includes spaces.

For example <title>The Anarchist Cowboys – American punk rock</title>

Here you've listed the name of your band clearly (The Anarchist Cowboys), and you've specified the style or description so people searching the term "American punk" or "punk rock" are more likely to find you. Your influences or an original phrase can also be added to the description. Just keep it concise. A full html example follows:

<title>**Title of Your Webpage Here**</title>
(bolded for emphasis)
<meta name="**description" content**="
Brief description of the contents of the page">
<meta name="**keywords**" content="
keyword phrases that describe your webpage">

The main search engines you will need to be listed on are:
Google (www.google.com/addurl/?continue=/addurl)
Yahoo (http://search.yahoo.com/info/submit.html)
MSN
(http://search.msn.com/docs/submit.aspx?FORM=WSDD2)
These sites generate the results for all the primary search engines. Dmoz (www.dmoz.org/add.html) feeds thousands of smaller search engines so be sure to sign up there too.

Don't waste your money on services promising to provide submissions to thousands of search engines. They won't help much, and they'll probably get you penalized by Google before long.

Things that will attract search engine traffic include a site index, footers, and XML feeds. Frames repel them. This is another reason to either go with a service like Wordpress, HostBaby or Bandzoogle. They will help you create a simple, search engine friendly website.

Hiring a webmaster is a great option. Like I said before though, just tell them you don't need all the bells and whistles (flash is not necessary! It will hurt you more than it will help you). You want a website that's simple and will attract people. The last thing you want is your new potential fan being bombarded with unasked for music and digital chaos when clicking on your site link.

Choose effective and clear keywords. (Free music, metal band, heavy metal music, etc) Be sure to mention these terms on your site to strengthen them. Don't go crazy with irrelevant choices either (Kim Kardashian photos, Disney movie clips, Paris Hilton, etc). There are many books dedicated solely to the topic of search engine optimization. "Search Engine Optimization for Dummies" by Peter Kent is a good one. Information found online or via these books can be a big help, but for now, as long as we choose the proper keywords, label our site correctly, and submit to the proper search engines we should be off to a good start.

To find out how to improve your Google page ranking, go to www.google.com/support.

Link Exchanges:

Although link exchanges can easily become a core part of your online marketing strategy, but they are not absolutely necessary. More and more, this technique is being overshadowed by simple, clean websites that allow for viral movement. Bands reciprocate with media and fan support by posting press pieces and messages of gratitude through social media. The more places you are on the web, the easier it is for people to find you, or 'stumble across' you. For the benefit of those who want to explore link exchanges, I'll include the below information.

Make It Easy For Others To Link To You:

Have a page that displays a variety of different banners and embeddable widgets (from Bandcamp, Soundcloud, and CDBaby) that webmasters and bloggers can place on their sites. Give them the option to place ready-to-paste html in their pages. This can add some incentive where there was none before, as it is much quicker to cut and paste code.

So who do you want to exchange links with? Well, try going to Google's top lists (http://www.google.com/Top/ or Alexa.com and search for the best by category. Let's explore this a bit more. So if you are an industrial band, you want to go to http://www.google.com/Top/Arts/Music/Styles/R/Rock/Industrial

See how many of these sites you can exchange links with and/or gain coverage on (I'll go over that later). Next, look in the other categories related to your niche.

http://www.google.com/Top/Arts/Music/Styles/R/Rock/Indu strial/Bands_and_Artists/

http://www.google.com/Top/Arts/Music/Styles/R/Rock/Indu strial/Radio/

http://www.google.com/Top/Arts/Music/Styles/R/Rock/Indu strial/Personal_Pages/

Have some rock in your sound too? Great. Then there are more options. Exploit your niches. Sure, this may not sound like much fun but it will be rewarding when you see your website traffic skyrocket. Websites with a higher Google ranking will help your own site ranking improve. Therefore, you should try to get your link posted or gain coverage (my preferred choice) on as many high-ranking websites as possible. If a site looks horrible and is difficult to navigate, it's best to skip and move on. You don't need to be associated with poor quality. Some sites hide multiple links sections in order to trade more often. My rule is - if it's difficult for you to find the links section from the front page, how is anyone else going to find it? It's not worth it. Also, there is no need to submit your link to free link directories or any similar programs.

Of course, you also want to offer links to radio shows or podcasts that play your music and websites or magazines that review your music. This is part of being at the bargaining table and having something to offer them. Build those relationships!

FREE AS A BIRD

Free music online can either spread like wildfire or sink like a stone. It largely depends on the work put into promotional efforts. Many bands post their album for free and think "I'm done! Our album is free and available, and who wouldn't want a free album?"

Well, first of all... those who don't know about it. If you want to generate those downloads, you'll have to put the hours in spreading the word. Artists who obsess over where their next 99 cents is going to come from (will it be Aunt Jackie or possibly your friend Dave?) may be unaware of this, but there is a major underground support network for artists who release free music. Much of this promotion machine is completely unavailable to artists who don't give up the good, so to speak.

At the top of the free music heap is the Free Music Archive, which you can find at www.freemusicarchive.org. The FMA describes itself as "an interactive library of high-quality, legal audio downloads." Directed by renowned freeform radio station WFMU and featuring a host of influential curators such as KEXP, KBOO, and CASH Music, the Free Music Archive has been featured in just about every major publication, and the artists they choose to cover get serious word-of-mouth. All songs shared within the FMA are shared through some sort of Creative Commons license, allowing it to be spread further through podcasts, Mp3 blogs, and other means. Many artists provide easy ways to connect with them for further permissions such as remixes, video use, or commercial use.

How do artists get their music considered? Visit www.freemusicarchive.org/contact for more information. The typical method is to email artists@freemusicarchive.org with the URL of the music you'd like to share, and if there is a particular FMA curator who may enjoy your work. If you have trouble hearing back, don't worry. Just try another method. Why not contact the curator's directly and personally? Keep track meticulously and follow up.

There are also thousands of free music blogs on Blogger.com, and Blogspot.com that post free albums after receiving permission from the artist or record label representative to post the zip file/album link. Now there's an idea. Most people are unaware of this, but many independent record labels will release an album and promote it through iTunes and physical record stores, while also promoting heavily to the underground market by spreading their own zip files and torrents to the appropriate channels.

This is smart, because, although I hate to be the bearer of bad news, the people who steal your music were not potential buyers anyway. Why not provide content to allow your music to spread like the latest drug on the underground market? Free music should be provided to major torrent sites, like Isohunt.com and Thepiratebay.se. A recent list of the top ten most popular torrent sites can be found here: http://torrentfreak.com/top-10-most-popular-torrent-sites-of-2012-120107/

Why not supply your music to them all? To cover ground on Blogger and Blogspot it can be trickier. It's going to take some serious digging. I recommend strapping yourself to a chair in front of your computer and searching terms like "free music downloads" along with "rock", "post-rock", "hip hop", or whatever your chosen genre is, and then adding site:blogspot.com or site:blogger.com to the search. You can do this under Google's regular web search and also under its blogs search, which I've found to be highly useful as well.

When you find a great site that suits your genre, this is where the fun begins. You're about to go off on a tangent, because Google is not your only friend. Blogrolls are your friends, and very close ones at that! Check out http://elementaryrevolt. blogspot.com/, for example, to get started and see what I mean. The first thing you want to do when finding a new blogs is check to see if your music fits, and then find the contact section. Once

[47]

you've contacted the webmaster with your music pitch, scroll down on their website to see the wealth of resources contained in the blogroll. Usually this will contain a series of other blogs catering to the same genre or genres of music, each with their own blogroll leading to more and more quality websites. Even if a blog has a small following, they're still worth contacting. Don't judge blogs simply on their Google followers or Facebook fans. Many frequenters of blogs don't sign up in any way. They simply take advantage of the content offered.

This is really a topic that could warrant a full book in itself, but the main intention here is to open your eyes to the underground market not usually mentioned in music marketing guides, and inspire you to start exploring. Experiment with different search terms until you're confident that you've looked under every stone that may have a free music blog servicing your genre underneath.

A better starting point, perhaps, is a free music blog directory arranged by genre at The Music List: http://themusiclist.net/. This should be a great aid in your search.

My favourite free music site is Totally Fuzzy, which links to album streams of both major and independent artists and has a large following. The site looks very professional, maintains a high level of quality control, and provides a powerful platform for musicians of all levels. Check them out here:

http://totallyfuzzy.blogspot.ca/

A helpful article with some further resources on promoting free music is at www.mashable.com/2011/02/06/free-legal-music.

Social Exchanges and the Middle Way:

The idea of giving your music away has its share of critics, just like anything else. Some say that the downside of giving your music away with no exchange is that the relationship ends there. While cases like The Weeknd have shown that to not always be the case, there is a middle way that bands can certainly walk, gaining most of the benefit of free and paid releases. Artists can supply their music to digital retailers for those who want to buy, and also provide their music to the free music blogs and torrents for those who don't. On top of this, there are social exchanges available, such as Bandcamp's "album for an email" option. No real fan is going to get mad at seeing "pay what you want" on your Bandcamp page after, say, buying your album on iTunes or CDBaby.

Promote all options at the same time to give your music the furthest reach to the most people. There are even apps such as Cash Music, who have a "Tweet for an mp3" social media mini-app that can be downloaded here:

http://cashmusic.org/tools/social/.

Why not offer bonus tracks to anyone who shares your album link? Perhaps everyone who tags you in a post advertising your music to their Facebook friends gets entered into a contest?

PRESS RELEASES

In the music business, the press release (or news release) is one of the most common tools used to bring an artist free publicity. It's a great way to let people know about your new CD, a tour, free downloads you are offering (keep this in mind – it will get you hits to your site), a label signing, or anything newsworthy that your band is doing. The more newsworthy your press release is the more exposure you will get.

Format is just as important as your content. A poor presentation, or typos, show a lack of professionalism and drastically reduces your chances the release will run as written, or at all for that matter. If submitting the press release by email, make sure to copy it into the body of the message rather than include it as an attachment. Attachments are a big no-no in the industry when you haven't yet built a rapport. Also, not everyone uses the same programs to view these documents.

What is a press release?

Basically, a press release is a simple sheet that provides news and information to editors, dj's, reporters, music fans and individuals in the press. The main thing to keep in mind is it has to be newsworthy. Make sure it reads like a news release rather than an advertisement. What's your angle? Don't worry – there are LOTS of them.

If your band donates funds from merchandise or CD sales to Amnesty International, for example, human rights organizations may be interested in distributing your news and even discussing your music with you. This could lead to interviews and more press coverage, but we're getting off track here. If your band covered a classic Metallica song, well you'd better make sure your press release gets out to all the Metallica fan forums and that you contact all the fan sites and blogs for coverage. Make sure to include your press release in the email.

[50]

Maybe one of the songs on your album is about something controversial. Do you praise or insult a public figure? Maybe one of your songs is a simple homage to small town America.

There Is A Market For Everything:
What your music is about will determine the audience who is interested in it. Every style has its own distributors. In general, you may want to pay a bit for Billboard's specialized service at www.billboardpublicitywire.com in order to spread your press release. Mi2n.com also has some specialized press release distribution services. These are good options for all genres. If you are a metal or heavy rock band, it's a good idea to submit your press releases to www.blabbermouth.net, for example, because they are highly influential. Once they accept it and you search your press release on Google, you'll notice within the week that many other metal and similar websites have posted your release as well. If this isn't actionable for you, simply insert your style and go to it!

Learn To Use Google To Your Advantage:
It's amazing how many bands don't investigate the leading media, or 'voices', in their genre. Google your style along with the word 'news' and see what comes up. Start a Microsoft Excel document and list all the relevant websites that report rock music news, country news, hip hop news, or whatever. You should include a column for the relevant contact name, email address, website address, phone number (if needed), date contacted, follow up date, and notes. This is the same document you should use to track your music submissions.

Examples of notes could be "John prefers darker rock tracks" or "Rock Magazine added us to their mixtape in July 2011. Ask for video premiere." This is your starting point. Want another trick? Try searching the term "submit news" (in quotes) along with "rock music" (or your chosen style). You will find tons of results leading you directly to news submission pages. You can also try terms such as "Send your news here" and "Send news tip". Keep making slight changes to both the style description and the news submission term and you will get new results. Add the relevant ones to your document as you go. Don't forget to send that news release as well.

This is how you start learning shortcuts and work smarter, not harder. As in martial arts, so with music!

So how do you write a press release?

Start it off with this:

"FOR IMMEDIATE RELEASE" (or FOR RELEASE JULY 1, 2010) and "For more information, contact:" Then you need to include your contact information: It must be a proper number, so the press can call to possibly offer you an interview.

Write Your Headline:

The headline is the only part of the release that should be in capitals. It also must be interesting so people pay attention and decide to bother reading your release and potentially check out your band. Don't be scared of controversy. "LOUISIANA ROCK BAND SLAMS OBAMA" looks more eye-catching than "LOUISIANA ROCK BAND SPEAKS THEIR MINDS". Why?

Well, because unfortunately not many people care if you speak your mind or not. Everyone speaks his or her mind all the time. People are just interested in getting their own two cents in. It's a sad truth. That being said, if you speak your mind on something THEY care about, you can bet they'll be checking the press release with a fine tooth comb! "What did they say about Obama? Who are these guys?" Now we're not suggesting that you insult Barack Obama of course. This is just an example.

The Body:

The body of your press release will include the simple details of your story. The first paragraph should grab the reader's interest and clearly explain the headline. Make sure you share what the news is and present it in a 3rd person style (he, she, the band, etc). Do not make the language overly promotional! For example, don't say "The Filthy Speed Demons, currently the best thrash metal band in the world, recently finished their new CD "All Hail the Filthy Speed Demons", which is sure to climb the charts rapidly." Be more objective!

Make sure it's proper and complete because many publications will run your press release verbatim. You can add quotes to make the release more interesting. This is a great idea to insert a comment on your new album or your latest benefit show.

Throw in potent keywords when relevant. Don't just add Angelina Jolie's name to your release if she has nothing to do with your music. However, if you wrote a song about Angelina, you may be on your way to a healthy amount of news coverage.

At the end of the release, summarize your story and add any "About Us" information that you think is necessary. "More information on the Filthy Speed Demons can be found at www.filthyspeeddemons.com." Finish it up with a contact for further information.

End your press release with the symbol "###" (without the quotation marks) after your last lines of text. This lets the editor know they have successfully received the entire release. It's really that simple.

FOR IMMEDIATE RELEASE
For more information, contact:
Your Name
Your Street Address
City, State, Zip Code
Phone
Fax
Email
HEADLINE:
MONTH DAY#, YEAR (CITY, STATE)

This is the who, what, where, when, and why. Make sure the first paragraph summarizes your news clearly.

Add additional details:

About The Band: (additional information)

For further information, contact Your Name at (xxx) xxx-xxxx. So now you've got your press release done. We mentioned some ways to distribute your release. Put some time into your research. It will be worth it. You basically want it to show up in as many places as possible. Don't underestimate the power of a strong press release.

Build Relationships:

Another thing I've been hinting at, but haven't talked about in depth – Build relationships! Keep tabs on who posted your release and create a document for yourself with the emails and websites who helped you. Call it your "list of allies" or something similar. You'll be surprised how fast it grows if you thank those people and publications.

In many cases, simply sending an email to thank a particular website or magazine for publishing your release can have a dual purpose. You can thank them for "supporting you in the past" and publishing your news releases, and ask for an interview or a CD review to "further the relationship". Be sure to say something like "Please let me know anything you need" and be ready to post banners and links, provide high quality photos and bio information – anything they need. Also, when you approach publications with your press release, don't spam them! Contact them individually by introducing yourself and possibly commenting on their writing or their publication. Let them know you're a real person. Remember, press releases are part of building relationships and they are part of the bait to generate even more press for your band.

Press Release Distribution – Never Automate!

We have established that it's a good part of any promotion strategy to have a good, concise, fact-based press release (or news release). We've also established that the best places to send that release are those that specifically ask for it through online submission forms as well as dedicated emails for the purpose of news tips (many publications have these).

However, it should be known that press releases are not meant to be distributed everywhere using impersonal methods. There are dozens of services aimed at independent musicians advertising press release distribution and/or music promotion. These include Beatwire.com and Musicsubmit.com, and of course, many others. I have tested both services and neither yielded any results. This is a simple fact, and of course, it may not be the case for everyone. I would warn any musician to stay away from these types of services, because even if they promise to send your press release to 10,000 contacts, you can be just about guaranteed that the emails are considered spam.

Of course, artists typically think "If my music is sent to that many people, at least 10 percent are bound to love it." This just isn't the case. In many cases, releases sent through companies like these will go COMPLETELY ignored, because there is no quality control at the starting point. So sending impersonal press releases to people's inboxes is not the way. Knowing this to be a fact, it should save you a lot of mistakes and a lot of wasted money. Distribution to online sources, however, can be a good thing and it can certainly help you appear more frequently in Google searches. For a list of press release distribution services from an independent review source, check out this link:

http://www.topseos.com/rankings-of-best-press-release-distribution-services

There is nothing wrong with paying for press release distribution either. Just make sure it's distributed online, and not involved with spamming of any kind. No one is going to discover your band in a personal junk folder!

For a distribution service specific to the music industry, one company that I have had positive experiences with is Mi2N - http://www.mi2n.com/. Created in 1998 by Eric de Fontenay, the company has consistently offered good services and even has a free option that is well worth it for independent artists. They have a range of paid distribution services that I would encourage artists

[55]

to try out and track the results. Mi2N is the largest online daily newswire serving the music industry. They promote press releases, music, and music videos, offering unique packages for each.

What's the point?

If we're straight talking and down to brass tacks here, the main point of a press release is to clearly and concisely communicate what's new with your band and why it's significant. If you use too much promotional language it will have the opposite effect you hope for, and you may even get a result sometimes considered worse than being ignored. You could get made fun of in a published review!

Your release should be helpful to the person reading it. Their research should be done for them, and no Googling or investigation should be necessary. It's as simple as that.

Inflated Expectations:

Since most of us read news releases when they're on a popular website or perhaps the newspaper, this context has taught us to see news releases as a powerful communication tool, which they certainly are when used correctly. However, it's very important to not have any expectations when distributing your news release. For the most part, independent artists will mainly see more of a cumulative, search engine/keyword benefit from the use of news releases, and not any kind of instant fame. In other words, don't sign up for press release distribution and wait for the phone calls to come pouring in. Keep moving in all directions. This advice applies to everything you do as an independent musician.

MY STRATEGY OF BEHIND-THE-SCENES MARKETING

Well, that's one of the main reasons you bought the book, isn't it? Here's the thing. I've scoured the net and a lot of articles on this topic are missing the mark. Yes, you can choose to hire a PR firm if you have the funds. If you choose to do so, there are good companies who run successful press campaigns for independent artists. Alternatively, if you're willing to work at it, you can certainly generate a ton of press yourself. Let's go through a few methods rarely described elsewhere. In fact, this one in particular is one of my original ideas. My advice is that you use it right away and count the results.

Be personal and/or stroke the ego.

Don't Always Go Through The Main Channels:

That could well be the most important sentence in this book. How do you get ahead in this world? Do you wait in line for everything? How about when the line is 1,000 people long? Some artists take longer than others to realize it but you must, and I'll repeat this often, BUILD RELATIONSHIPS.

If someone knows nothing about you and you offer him or her nothing in return, there is about a 1/100 chance they will cover your music. That works fine if you want to send 1,000 emails to get potentially 10 reviews and burn a lot of bridges in the meantime.

Being personal means more than just copying and pasting the person's name into your pre-written email template. Of course, the press release or album information part of your email can be pre-written. The rest should be original and engaging. Anyone who runs a podcast, or writes for a music publication, is bombarded by bands on a regular basis. You have the opportunity to either make someone's day or aggravate them.

[57]

Ask yourself what typically makes your day as an independent musician? It could very well be that one email you get from a fan who appreciates your music. Maybe they have a particular favourite song and they tell you why. You think "This person actually listened to me". This is the same feeling you want the independent press to get when they read your emails.

If you write the typical "Check out my band" email, it's the equivalent of people posting their advertisements on your Facebook wall.

What can you do to build the relationship?

What we're trying to say is: If you are a metal band and you go to the Google listing of Top metal websites (http://www.google.com/Top/Arts/Music/Styles/R/Rock/Heavy_Metal/) you may be tempted to immediately go to their contact sections and follow their submission policies verbatim. For some of these websites, that would certainly be the best route, but remember, music marketing, just like music creation, is an intuitive process.

We're going to go through this in great detail since it's critical and it seems nobody else covers the topic in too much depth.

Sometimes going by the rules doesn't pay. You may submit all of your CD's to a popular publication year after year and never get a review – or any coverage at all. This is when you change your tactic.

The media are not so intimidating. They are just groups of individuals! Therefore, when you can, contact them INDIVIDUALLY. This is how you get into 'the fortress'. When we say the fortress, we refer to a popular music website, magazine or publication.

Contact INDIVIDUALS. The media is a lot less scary when we realize that they are all just collectives of individuals. Independent music media is even easier to crack. Most of the reviewers don't get paid much (if at all) and they are music fans like you. How intimidating is that? That means they have something in common with you. Use that to your advantage.

Tactic 1) Embrace the Ego:

Try looking up articles on YOUR favourite bands, or most importantly, bands that are similar in style to your own - and contact the person who wrote the piece. Reviews on niche bands give you something unique to talk about. You can relate to the writer about being one of the few people to discover the band. Even better, congratulate them on discovering the band in question!

Say something personal about the review/article - why you liked it, what you like about the band, etc. Be natural. Ask a question such as "Have you heard such-and-such a band? I think you'd love them." This gets a conversation started. Keep in mind these writers typically get no feedback from their reviews and articles so positive feedback or a pat on the back will get their attention. In the title of the email mention who the email is attention to and how you found them.

For example "Attn Sean – your Queens of the Stone Age review". Guaranteed that will get Sean's attention. It looks much better than "Attn reviews – Please review my band!" Count on those to go to the delete box more often than not. In the SECOND paragraph, you mention your band. Don't be pushy. Provide a website link, or better yet, have a digital download of your album sent to their email address. (Bandzoogle and HostBaby should have this capability. Use it! It will save you money.)

Here is a template for you to get an idea. Keep in mind the idea is to be honest and actually communicate with this person. Change your wording every time! Try to genuinely relate to the writer.

HEADER: "Attn Sean – Your Queens of the Stone Age review"

BODY: "Hi Sean, This is James from the rock band Broken Jaw Dance Party. I found ____ Magazine through your rather excellent review of Queens of the Stone Age's album "Lullabies to Paralyse". I thought it was well done and agree with your favourite track choices (mine are "Little Sister" and "Burn the

Witch" as well). I'm curious as to what you think of their latest release "Era Vulgaris". To me it's a stronger album. Also, have you heard (insert band name here)? Given your musical preferences you may get into them. Check them out and let me know what you think.

I've sent you a digital copy (email the digital copy of the album to Jame's email address. It should arrive as a free download that he can access easily) of Broken Jaw Dance Party's new album "Curbstomp Disco", as I think you'd enjoy it. Queens are a big influence of ours (give a short story of how you got into them, or keep it simple) and a review would be appreciated of course.Thanks for your time and once again, great job on the review!

Sean

Broken Jaw Dance Party

www.brokenjawdanceparty.com

(include email and phone number contact in signature)

Tactic 2) Make a Friend:

We encourage you to check out "Staff" sections on music websites. Many music websites will have an area where they provide a list of their staff with email addresses, photos, music preferences, hobbies etc. Find someone you relate to and email these people! Once again – have a conversation first and foremost. Many writers will even ignore great artists if the artist doesn't take the time to engage them. Ask yourself, "What is a blog post worth to me?" If it's worth $5, $10, $20 or even $50, it's definitely worth some deep thought and a conversation.

As with conversation, so with emailing. Nothing gets people to light up more than to talk about what they're interested in with the knowledge that someone is really listening. The blogger wants to be appreciated for their blogs the same way you want to be appreciated for your music. Once you understand that, you can start working on that premise.

Tactic 3) Support the Media:

Independent media is at once thriving and collapsing. You would be surprised how much it helps when you retweet a review, share it on Facebook, or suggest it on Pinterest. It makes you look good to the place that supported you and opens the door to further coverage, and at the same time spreads your music to new potential fans by making your name more visible. It also exposes more people to the publication, making them more able to influence the success of deserving bands. Help them help you!

Tactic 4) Drop the unfounded negativity:

Somewhere along the line, the general perception of music reviewers, at least from the musician's standpoint, became extremely negative. This is the same thing that has happened generally with the music industry. It's a "no one is throwing me a bone" mentality.

Seeing both sides of the coin, I have to say that musicians tend to show more ignorance when it comes to not realizing that no one owes them anything, especially time. It takes time to read your bio. It takes time to listen to your music. It definitely takes time to write about your music. Considering 99 percent of the people who write about music do it for the love of it without pay, it stands to reason that they should be respected, and that they are really no different from musicians. It's merely a perceptual divide. Drop those misconceptions. They will only divide you from others. Fix that up and all of a sudden you are connected with another human being who is just like you.

Tactic 5) Include All Information In A Concise Format:

This is a general tip that applies to all music submissions. Many artists and PR companies either make their media pitches way too long or way too short. I have opened up emails that go on for pages or contain endless unwanted attachments. I also have received emails that only contain a zip file or one or two sentences and no artist link. These swiftly go to the junk folder.

Here is a template that I use when submitting music for review consideration.

(Personal message at the top w/optional press release below)
Artist name:
Location:
Styles:
CD name:
Release date:
Label information:
Streaming Link:
Secure Music Download Link:
Secure Press Photos Link:
Tracklisting:
Production details:
Members/Instruments:
Websites:
Music video links:
Press contact:
Artist contact:
Highlights/Accolades:
Bio:

Notes on this template:

For your Streaming link, Soundcloud, Bandcamp or your own private link are perfect for this purpose. Soundcloud includes a feature that allows you to set up your whole album for streaming, and even create private links that allow easy downloads of your release.

Your album download link, or zip file, can be hosted on a service such as Mediafire.com, Yousend.com or Dropbox.com. Make sure there are no pop-up advertisements or other annoyances. Put yourself in the shoes of the person on the other end of your email. To make it easiest on the media, I usually create a zip file containing the high quality version of the album (320 kbps), the album cover art (a large, high quality version), 4 or 5 high quality band photos, and a professional one-sheet or document with bio and contact information in case they lose the original email. This ensures that you're not burying anyone with too many zip files, although it's generally fine to have two.

When it comes to listing similar artists, a common mistake is to aim too high. Want a helpful tip? Don't choose Radiohead. If you say you sound similar to Radiohead, your email may get skipped. Only Radiohead sounds like Radiohead, and it's usually not a good move to pinpoint an act that so many people connect with on such a deep level. Acts like Metallica and U2 are also too big to list as similar artists. I know that when I receive music submissions with comparisons like this, it just doesn't register on my psyche for some reason. However, if names like The Melvins, A Place to Bury Strangers, Django Django or Charles Bradley get mentioned, it peaks my interest.

Try choosing a mid-level "hip" band who are currently frequenting the music blogs, SXSW festival, CMJ, etc. Make sure you are sonically similar, of course. You will get more results comparing yourself to Cloud Nothings than Nirvana, for example. Make sense?

For the websites section, don't list every social media site or musician's community you have a page on. Just include your official website, Facebook, Twitter, Soundcloud, Bandcamp, Last.fm and Youtube pages.

The style section should be thought of the same way as the similar artists section. It's meant to generate interest in your music, so instead of just 'alternative rock', you may have better luck with 'alternative rock, garage rock, indie rock'. It creates more of a sense of depth. Of course, make sure everything you list is relevant to your particular sound and influences.

For highlights and accolades, the whole purpose of this is once again to be helpful and appease the short attention span of the reader. This is not meant as any kind of insult. I happen to have short attention span myself. It's a fact of the internet age. People who take long periods of time away from their computers often report having unbelievable amounts of creativity and clarity return. In the time that I've been promoting music online, my attention span has diminished considerably. Therefore, a highlights and accolades section can be very helpful as a point form guide to why your band should be covered.

What should you include here? Have you opened for any notable bands? Have you won any awards? Have you been covered in any respectable publications or popular blogs? Is there anything strange or unique about you? If you are just starting out, you may not need this. You can always add to it later.

Remember: The personal touch works for interviews too.

If one of the person's interests is politics, you could say "My band wrote a song about the current financial crisis. Maybe we could do an interview for your publication and discuss this." (Just an example. It may be difficult to write an interesting song about the financial crisis!)

The whole idea is – when you visit a website; think to yourself "Someone who writes for this site will relate to me". Think of it as making a new ally or friend. One thing that's hard for musicians to understand sometimes is that we're all music fans. It's not all about the musician. Bands that simply send out mass emails asking media (and fans for that matter) to "check out our album" do not get nearly the results that bands who express interest in who they are writing to.

Find something you are genuinely interested in about the person's opinions or ideas. If you can't find anything at all, maybe you should go the main route.

Tactic 6) The Normal Route Done Right:

What is the normal route? The normal route is going to the website or publication's "contact" or "FAQ" section and finding out their submission procedures. Do everything they ask. If they require a physical CD, don't send a digital download. Follow the protocol. Then send a quick, polite email to the main email provided introducing yourself and letting them know that your CD is on the way. Thank them for the opportunity and let them know you are keen to get involved with their site and are happy to cross promote as well. Be polite, thankful and helpful!

Many blogs will have dedicated music submission emails. For these, you can use the template shared previously unless they specify otherwise. Some will have online forms requesting specific information. Always provide what they ask for, and if they request no follow ups, take note of that as well.

Make a note of the email, publication, and date of contact in a document such as a Microsoft Excel sheet, and follow up if required in 3-4 weeks. Many times you will get an individual reply to your first email, so you will have an INDIVIDUAL to follow up with. See how it all comes together?

Remember, you'll need to use more than one tactic to generate reviews. Some larger websites do not display any contact information for their staff. You will have to be vigilant. Follow up!

Tactic 7) Become a Stalker:

Please note that this title is meant to be humorous and I in no way advocate any kind of harassment.

Here's the deal. There is no easy way to get your band featured in major publications such as Pitchfork, NME or Rolling Stone. Seeking out freelance writers and contributors can be a way to get in the door. You can find them through creative Google searches and appeal to them by getting personal through email. Check Blog Critics, Examiner.com, Technorati.com, About.com or Suite 101 and get in touch with the writers there. Many writers for major blogs such as Pitchfork, the Aquarian Drunkard and Stereogum are freelance writers who write for a variety of publications.

Also, most professional writers have their own blogs, Twitter accounts, and Linkedin profiles where their contact information is accessible. When you contact them, be polite and clear as to your intentions, and don't take much of their time. There's nothing wrong with "finding" someone as long as their information is readily available, they are treated with respect, and you only ask once.

Tactic 8) Become A Donor:

I bet you haven't heard that one before, hey? I hear so many musicians say their main complaint is that they contacted hundreds of music blogs and barely received any response. However, in their quest for press, they were so focused on bloggers and writers helping them that they never thought of helping the bloggers. As you scour the blogosphere and find blogs that seem like they would be a perfect match for your music, you'll notice that many of them have a Paypal donation button. If you respect the blog, why not donate $5 or $10, and then submit your music for consideration? You'd be extremely surprised at the results.

I once donated $10 to a blog I was impressed by, and they were so appreciative that they wrote an article about me, saying I was the first person to bother donating in the past 2 years they had been a music blog. It's a way of telling someone that you respect their publication and that you're not only thinking about yourself. My rate of reviews when I donate to a blog is almost 100 percent, provided the blog/artist combination is appropriate.

If a band were to budget $500 towards donations, I would wager that it would have a much more significant effect than most advertising options.

Tactic 9) Set Up Shop And Barter:

There are many reasons why independent artists don't get covered. Sometimes the email gets lost in a sea of thousands of others. Sometimes the blogger is overwhelmed and just doesn't have the time. Sometimes it's not worth their time. This is just the honest truth. Luckily, there are multiple ways of making it worth someone's time, and you just have to judge the situation to find out what that is.

Why not set up your own music blog? It only takes a few hours. Go to www.wordpress.com and choose a template. Then create content by publishing 10 articles or so. From there, start networking and exchanging blogroll links with small blogs. Once you're rolling, you now have something to offer other bloggers and webmasters; a platform with value (provided you've put an honest effort into building your blog). While most blogs are completely uninterested in exchanging links with bands, they are almost obsessive about exchanging links with other blogs. If you can't beat them, join them. Offering a blogroll or banner link as well as cross-promotion through your social networks is a good way to get coverage.

Mutual benefit is very much the way the music industry works. It's your responsibility to make powerful music, and it's the bloggers responsibility to only post good music, so any betrayal of either aspect leaves the blame resting firmly on the individual. Having something to offer means you have more tools at your disposal. Pretending there's any sort of level playing field in the music industry or in life doesn't do anyone any justice. You need to be great, but also treat it like a business.

Blogroll exchanges typically work best with small to mid-level publications. You won't want to bother offering this to Stereogum, for example. Use traditional methods for larger outlets.

Another way to do this is to set up your own PR company. After reading this book, you'll have just about all the tools you need. Once again, Wordpress is your friend. You can either run the PR company yourself or outsource the work to qualified individuals. It really doesn't matter as long as the work is done properly. This is an ideal option if you have the time but you don't have the money. Many music blogs and publications prefer being contacted by a PR company.

The added bonus is this. While most PR companies work with between 10 -30 clients at any given time, you'll be working with just one. This means that when you offer cross-promotion and submit the music, you're not asking for much on their end. If they simply post your Soundcloud link, their work is done, and now they have a new affiliate. With one artist, your efforts don't get diluted at all. If more PR companies could focus on just one artist while using this tactic, they could come very close to breaking the right artist. The amount of press would be staggering.

Tactic 10) Paid reviews:

This is another controversial one, for a few specific reasons which I'll identify, and, in my own view, overcome. Many people have an issue with paid reviews because they imagine that there is some sort of level playing field, or that there should be, and that paid reviews don't give the next musician a chance. The other issue that some people have is the idea of quality control. Pay-per-review sites that accept everyone can end up being review dumps, and nobody wants that.

The level playing field argument is a bit hypocritical. Many publications will respond to PR companies and artists' emails with advertising rate sheets. In some cases, buying advertising is a sure way to get coverage... very expensive coverage. In other cases, publications claim that the two aren't connected, but you can be pretty sure that if you don't buy advertising you won't get reviewed. This is only in some cases, and I mention it to illustrate the point. I can see why larger publications don't do this, but more small and mid-level publications may begin offering more ambitious plans in the future as an alternative to advertising, and a way to support the publication. While I don't agree with "pay-for-consideration" models, I do feel that paying for only approved, high quality artists could make for a functional system. Most music blogs are so inundated with requests they have no motivation to even check their email. It's a broken system. Having an option such as this solves that problem and gives the blog longevity.

Why shouldn't writers get paid for their work? Small and mid-level blogs sometimes appreciate the support of their writers as well, and advertising is not the only way it should be coming in.

What I've been referring to here is rooted in the building of relationships, and acting from intuition and trust. There are also other, easier options when it comes to paid reviews, and they should be used as helpful tools as well.

Fiverr.com, for example, is a very popular micro-job website where every job on the site costs only $5. Set up an account and link it with your Paypal, and you're ready to start shopping. Using their handy search function, you'll find everything from music reviews and podcast spots to interviews and music video promotion. There are a few tricks I've learned about using Fiverr effectively.

a) Fiverr is not a total solution. Many artists find Fiverr, think it's the holy grail, and perhaps their ticket to fame. However, Fiverr should be a small part of an artist's overall promotion strategy, not all of it.

b) Be diligent. Some of the gigs offered on Fiverr are worthwhile and some are extremely poor. Ask to see the website before ordering your gig. Does it look ok? Would this be a sensible addition to your brand?

c) Keep checking for updates. I'd advise searching "music reviews", "music blog", and other similar search terms once every week or two. You'll find that new gigs pop up. Why is this important? I'll let you in on a little secret. While many people write off Fiverr completely, to do this would be a mistake. I won't name names, but some very significant publications have offered gigs through Fiverr in the past. Sometimes, they only last a month on the site, because the stress of receiving poor music submissions for only $5 can be unsustainable. This is what brings me to my next suggestion.

d) Maintain relationships. It's against Fiverr's code of conduct to exchange emails within the site. I highly recommend keeping an Excel document of relevant Fiverr gigs, though, and continue to add any valuable new ones that you find. Any gigs that get paused or perhaps deleted are usually because the publication no longer wishes to work within Fiverr's restrictions. It also typically means that the publication is at a level where they are getting good traffic. It's always a good idea to approach these publications with a better offer such as $10 or $15 to review your album. Just because they're tired of doing reviews for $5, it doesn't mean they don't want to be paid well for their work.

Other websites that offer paid opportunities are the common ones, Sonicbids.com and Musicxray.com. Many of these opportunities are on a "pay for consideration" model, so be diligent with these, and there's absolutely nothing wrong with contacting the publication outside of the website with a personal note or a phone call. If you're a real person to them and not just a music submission, it can make all the difference in the world.

More paid review services can be found through publications such as:

Skope Magazine (www.skopemag.com)
I Am Entertainment Magazine (www.iaemag.com)
Muzik Reviews (www.muzikreviews.com),
Music Emissions (www.musicemissions.com).

These are all worthwhile publications and definitely worth the price for a fair review. With these services being available as a platform for independent artists, there's no longer any excuse to have zero reviews for your new album.

Tactic 11) Build A Freelance Army:

Post an ad on Craigslist looking for quality freelance writers who want to write music reviews, features, and interviews, and are willing to pitch these pieces to various publications and blogs. Outsource reviews the same way you outsource advertising. Get people working on your behalf, because you'll find that not many people are going to take up your mantle for free.

You would be extremely surprised as to the quality of writers you'll hear from. Writers with multiple degrees, writers who contribute to top publications and magazines, you name it. There are no guarantees, but why not have them pitch your music to those publications? This is an inside track, and I'd go as far as to say it could be more lucrative than anything else you do promotion-wise.

If you prefer not to have the writer's shop the articles for you, there are literally hundreds of websites that accept user-generated content where you could submit them yourself.

Tactic 12) Advertising:

As I mentioned earlier, advertising can be critical to your success as an artist, not necessarily because people will click on the ads and find their new favourite band, but because the media are so heavily dependent on them that they appreciate a band who is forward-thinking enough to buy advertising. You'll need to do your research.

Blogs that are small enough to really notice your support are good choices, and it's also easier on the wallet, in some cases as low as $10-$20 per month for a banner ad. This is well worth it especially since you'll most likely be covered on the blog in this case. Other publications are more of a major decision, and will take some savings to get involved with. Good publications to consider advertising in include www.indiemusicreviewer.com, www.undertheradarmag.com and www.cmj.com.

Tactic 13) The user-generated revolution:

The music press has changed radically. Nowadays, you're more likely to read a music review or feature from a freelance or amateur contributor than a full-time writer. What does this mean for you? It means you can have a friend write a piece on your band and submit it to any music site allowing guest posts or guest bloggers. Even better; get professional freelancers to do this for you. Hit every site, and trust me, there are hundreds. For the benefit of the general public, make sure the pieces are actual editorial pieces, and not promotional advertisements. Simple blog posts are even better. The point is not to pollute the music media, but to set up your own quality freelance editorial street team and get your name out there to people who will enjoy your work.

Remember – The media are the opinion makers.

Finding out about new music through the media can take place through a review, feature, interview, blog post, or some sort of radio play or music sharing. If you respect the source, you will be more likely to buy or check out the artist. This goes for everything from Rolling Stone and NME to personal blogs and Facebook pages.

So whose opinion is worthwhile? It's all in the numbers. There are internet-only publications with readerships in the tens of thousands. You need to get your music to these people. Talk to them. Connect with them. Send your music to places such as Pitchfork Media and PopMatters.

Blogs have become extremely important in recent years, effectively taking over traditional media. Look up music blogs that cater to your style of music and contact the author in the Behind-the-scenes marketing style. Choose a tactic that suits the blog. This is time consuming, especially if you're just starting to build your contact list. No one said being your own publicist and doing it right was easy. Allow these blogs to share your music if they want to. If the right blog posts your album or talks about your band, it can go viral.

MUSIC BLOGS AND MUSIC DISCOVERY

While some artists set their minds on that feature article in Rolling Stone, the smart ones are emailing all the Music bloggers (within their relevant style) they can find. Music bloggers are freelance music reviewers who write and share the music they love online. They are usually quite independent though they can tend to have a lot of listeners/subscribers.

Many MP3 blogs do allow submissions, so submitting your music to get reviewed not only is great exposure for your music, but a good review will help you get blurbs for your press kit. Let your promotion feed itself. The more you get talked about, the more you have to post on your site networks and blogs. More people find you and the positive cycle continues.

Remember that the bloggers are the mouths that speak to today's music listener. If they talk about you in a positive light, you are on your way. We advise that you visit Hype Machine immediately and start searching the thousands of mp3 blogs to find where you fit in.

The Hype Machine:

For an overwhelming, but hopefully exciting list of music mp3 blogs that can post your music, go to http://hypem.com/list. The way the Hype Machine works is it tracks a huge amount of popular mp3 and music blogs – currently a handpicked listing of almost 800. The music blogs post music and the Hype Machine presents it on their own site so the public can find "all the best music in one place".

With an overarching goal of empowering independent voices that write about music, it's difficult to argue with their philosophy. You can search the blogs by genre or just go through them alphabetically. You can also search similar artists to your band on the Hype Machine's network, and choose to contact

[73]

those blogs only. This can get you a ton of new listeners, and it gives you something to talk about with the blogger.

The other fantastic feature of the Hype Machine is that the more popular your song grows on the network, the more other bloggers tend to pick it up and repost on their own blogs. Bloggers tend to want to write about what other bloggers writer about, so getting on the good side of this group of bloggers is essential to the success or obscurity of independent artists. Beyond the blogging community here, there is also a community of tastemakers over a million strong. They are a mixture of DJ's and music fans, and you can bet that they have their eyes peeled for the next new artist to grace the Hype Machine charts. Once a blog adds your music to the Hype Machine, members of the community then need to "heart" your music in order for it to get on the charts. It's important to seize the momentum and act right away. This is one of the rare cases where I advocate getting your friends and family to sign up for the Hype Machine and "heart" your music. If you can get on the charts, artists often find that things take a life of their own.

A whole book could be written on the merits of the Hype Machine, but let's just say it's important to our current musical landscape, and any independent artist would do well to look at it from a creative and "outside the box" perspective, taking time to get to know each and every blogger catering to their genre.

Elbows: Elbo.ws calls itself "the most comprehensive music blog aggregator", and it would be hard to argue that this is another blog community with a massive amount of influence. Elbo.ws is quite selective with its blogs, but its database is much larger than the Hype Machine's. It currently boasts a directory of over 4,000 music blogs. Users can look up popular blogs, tracks and videos to see what the current trends are. Like the Hype Machine, you can also search by artist if you're looking specifically for similar artists to your own band.

The name of the game is essentially the same as on the Hype Machine. The more blogs post about you, the higher you rise on the charts. With a directory over triple the size of the Hype Machine, Elbo.ws is not to be ignored. As you go through the blogs relevant to your band, remember to keep adding contact emails to your master excel document. It can be tedious work, but once it's done, you have a list that you can use for years.

Other quality music blog aggregators include Shuffler.fm and Wearehunted.com.

Technorati: Got more time on your hands? Technorati.com indexes over 11,000 music blogs last time I checked. If you want better than average results and new allies, try looking through the blog list in reverse. This will show you a series of blogs that either have just been added to the directory recently or are not popular enough yet to have a high ranking. Why would you want to do that? For one reason that I'll go into more later, you'll get a much better response ratio emailing blogs that get a few emails a day as opposed to 10,000. Also, in many cases, the blogger is appreciative that you reached out to them and noticed their blog.

Don't Rely on Blog Directories or Major Media:

The common thing for artists to do is look up a convenient list of the Top 50-100 music blogs, email them all and consider the job done. In fact, PR companies sell the same illusions to bands all the time by promising to send their music to all the major outlets. Pitchfork. Rolling Stone. NME. Stereogum. SPIN. Under the Radar. Sounds pretty good, right?

In fact, the illusion works pretty well. I have artists approach me all the time asking "Will you send my music to Rolling Stone?" This opens up a whole can of worms, but one way I can sum it up is this. Be where you are. Move from there. Should you send your album to Pitchfork according to their specifications? Absolutely. If they choose to review it, that would be a game changer. However, there's a problem with only targeting media that you personally read or find relevant. Chances are you're not relevant enough yet to be covered.

[75]

Why is it that we all want to skip the journey? We want to jump from the garage to Rolling Stone. You need to make major strides in your career for these top tier publications to even see you as a blip on their radar. Many artists ignore small blogs, even when they're small themselves. It makes no sense. To build momentum, you need to befriend people who are at your level of progress and find ways you can help each other. Never underestimate what a small blog can do for you.

First get your name out on the small and mid-level blogs. Then, the big blogs take notice. The blogosphere tends to be a world full of voyeurism and copycats. This means that when your name is repeatedly posted, it has a strong cumulative effect.

Many of these blogs you'll want to promote yourself to have not been listed with Technorati, and aren't in the chosen lists featured on Hype Machine or Elbows. I suggest searching various terms in Google's blogs search related to your genre, and you'd be surprised the quality of blogs that come up. Many have a decent following that has grown organically, but they're not considered hip enough for the other directories.

Don't Stick to Your Own Language:

In my searches through the various blog directories, I've inevitably found some sites that activate Google translate. This should give you some good ideas. With features this easy to use, you're free and clear to build contacts all over the world. Why not target German electronic music blogs, Swedish metal blogs, or Brazilian rock radio shows? Whatever your style, whatever your fancy, people are probably more keen on it outside of your local scene. A rock band may have trouble getting heard in North America, but Europe has a much stronger appreciation of rock, for example. When you find a site that is exactly what you're looking for, check their blogroll for the goldmine. Always document as you go so you don't have to go through this grueling process on your next album!

Does this take much time?

Sure. It will initially. But the results can be shocking. Do you want a press page filled with quotes from music publications raving about your band? That's the way to do it (provided your music is strong, of course). Get personal and use the correct tactic for the situation, and you will get those reviews coming in.

Reviews typically come in over a period of 1-6 months as well, which can be a good thing, as it can seem like Christmas when you check your inbox. Writers can tend to be busy people. This can mean that if you connect with enough people, you'll get a few efficient writers who provide you reviews within a few weeks. Remember – you are planting seeds. Don't let yourself get discouraged. You should be reaching out to thousands of people.

Now you've got your press page off to a good start. Be sure to get their permission before posting the review in full or in part on your website. If you've connected with enough people, you will continue to see reviews coming in over the next long while – people you forgot you contacted will be sending you reviews, and this keeps your band in the spotlight somewhat. Pat yourself on the back every time you get a positive review.

The best way to set up your press page is to list quotable press clippings as opposed to full reviews. Make sure you choose the most appealing lines, and hyperlink with credit to the original review. For example, something like this may create intrigue.

"Sarah and the Dreamweavers are the next rock act to take over England, without a doubt in my mind." – James Jacobs, London Rocks Magazine

"I was blown away by every aspect of this new British sensation." – Music Supreme Magazine

Allow yourself to celebrate because working, as an independent musician, is a series of small victories. With every review that arrives, you should be having a glass of wine and taking a moment to enjoy the success. Be thankful.

Can You Use Negative Reviews?

Yes and no. If the negative review goes something like "The instrumentation was subpar and the vocals were awkwardly bad. I felt embarrassed listening to this band. Boy, do they ever suck." then you probably would not want to post it on your website. It's bad enough that it's posted anywhere!

However, if the review goes something like "Where do these punks get off saying these terrible things about the government? The music was pure noise! It's immoral, un-American, and I don't know how people could listen to this musical chaos!", and you are an anarchist punk band or a politically charged heavy metal group, it's fair game and could very well work for you rather than against you. How much negative press have bands like Rage against the Machine gotten over years? It's only fueled the fires and made them look cooler to their fan base. Get the idea?

Negative comments on blog posts and message boards can be a very good sign, too, so don't get discouraged. A band that gets talked about is a band that is making waves. When you start making waves, some people are going to get annoyed. It's to be encouraged. People just love to share their opinions, even though opinions, of course, mean nothing when faced with reality.

Why do I use the term Behind-the-Scenes Marketing?

Now I've gone over some clear examples of what I call behind-the-scenes marketing (and other types of marketing) for independent bands. The reason I use the term behind-the-scenes marketing is because the viewing audience, the music fans, do not get access to your personalized emails or an unimpressive image of your lead singer sitting in front of a computer emailing away.

What the viewing audience will see is a "critically acclaimed" new band. It's that simple. Make friends who in turn create the frontline for you. You don't do it yourself. As I've said, if you call yourself "the next Nirvana", people will laugh. But if Revolver Magazine makes this claim about your band, you may just find that people rush to your website to hear your new album. Move behind-the-scenes in the dead of night and your flag just may be raised by morning.

NEWSLETTERS AND MAILING LISTS

A good option for your website is to have a visible mailing list or newsletter sign up. It's a good idea to capture their name and email address. Your band mailing list can quickly become one of your best marketing tools, and the ratio of people who actually read your content is much higher than Facebook. Both Bandzoogle and HostBaby will give you mailing list capability, and there are plenty of outside websites, such as www.mailchimp.com and www.awer.com that provide the same service and will manage an email list for you. If you hire a webmaster, they should be able to create a custom feature for you as well.

Newsletters, used effectively, are one of the best promotional tools a band can have, and they're typically free or very inexpensive. Make sure you are collecting names and email addresses at your live shows and events. Cover all fronts. If you are collecting emails through your website, your social networks, and your live shows, you'll have thousands of fans on your mailing list in no time.

What Should Be In Your Newsletter?

Well, that's up to you but there are guidelines that can help. It's a good idea to have an intro or even a table of contents in order to let people know what's coming. As far as content goes, there's the obvious –

News articles (possibly your latest press release)

Recent reviews (which you're overflowing with after following the steps in our reviews chapter, right?)

Interesting information about members of the band (you ARE interesting, aren't you?)

Fan comments (Quotes from fan feedback – for example "Thanks for the CD guys! Every song is amazing and it's been in my CD player all month!" – Sarah from Los Angeles)

Contests (I'll get more into the significance of contests later, but it's a great way to get people used to paying more attention to your mailing list)

Upcoming events (What's coming down the pipe?)

Something personal (This is optional. Possibly include a recent blog. People get turned off if your whole newsletter is sales based. Talk to them. Give them something original to read.)

Humour (Put it all together with humour. Don't be boring. Don't just give a sales pitch. Be a human being!)

Recognition for your allies (Post links to "friends of the band". This could be radio or podcasts who have played your music recently or a website that has covered your band. It's a way of saying thanks and getting more exposure for them. They will appreciate it.)

Your merchandise (What are you selling? You want to sell, don't you? Entice people to buy.)

Questions! You can ask your fans for feedback. What songs would they like to see you cover? What town would they like you to visit next? What song should you promote to radio next?

Exclusive content (Why not record a Youtube performance just for your biggest fans? How about releasing a b-side mp3 only for your subscribers? The more content, the better. Make it worth it for your fans to check their inboxes!)

Social network information (Make sure you include your social network information. You want to make sure everyone is signing up to strengthen your online presence.)

Unsubscribe information (Let people know they are not obligated to receive the newsletter.)

Does that give you some good ideas? Make sure you run a spell check. If you miss out on this some people will think you're unprofessional and cancel their subscription.

How Do You Build Your Mailing List?

There are many ways to build your mailing list. Here are a few ideas: **Advertise** it on your homepage and your social networks. **Create an incentive**. Have a contest. "Sign up for our mailing list and get a free mp3 download of our new single" or "Sign up for our mailing list and get entered into our ultimate prize pack contest". This could be a CD, poster and t-shirt, for example. **Be creative**. Send a lock of your bassist's hair. It's all up to you. Don't think of it as giving something away for free. After all, you're getting an email address and a potential future customer. They are giving you momentum, and that's priceless.

Collect email addresses at your live performances, as we mentioned earlier. Have a mailing list at your merchandise table and make sure you get an email address from anyone who buys a CD or compliments the band.

Get everyone in the band involved in building the list. Have each member gather email addresses from their co-workers, friends and family. It's important for the morale of the band to not let any member slack off. By promoting yourself, you're feeding the energy and excitement of your band. The more results you get, the more motivation you will have to move forward and see what's around the corner. **Advertise** your mailing list on your personal facebook. When you run into an acquaintance, ask for their email to include. Be aggressive.

NEVER add people to your mailing list without asking. You may think "this reviewer loved my music so he'll probably want to keep up on my news." This can turn someone who was previously a supporter into someone who cringes when they see your band name. Ask them first.

VIRAL MARKETING
(Why bother going viral?)

Advertising on the internet (through banner ads, pay-per-click, pop-up windows, and other ad marketing) has been producing worse and worse results. At this point, it's barely worth it for even large companies to go these routes. If you had a choice when watching television to sit through the advertisements or just watch the show's content, what would you choose? When watching television, you have to go by the rules, but on the internet, the user has control – and they absolutely do not want to see advertising. Marketers are spending more and more on traditional advertising methods to achieve a fraction of the result.

This does not necessarily mean that people have completely rejected the messages of marketing or advertising campaigns. After all, we all still buy products. It's simply the WAY that marketing products that has changed.

Most people prefer looking up specific things online – get what they want specifically and go. People will typically ignore anything that looks like advertising. Advertising may work in the physical world but not so much in the online world.

What's the solution? It's simple. Stop marketing AT people. Somehow, we need to get people marketing to each other. And when we do market, we need to be human about it. Make it engaging. Advertise through other people's words and mouths as opposed to your own. For example, product promotion has moved mainly to places such as word-of-mouth and social networks. People who frequent and contribute to these networks and websites act like advertisers in a lot of ways. They:

Spread the word about new products or services.

Communicate the incentives, features and potential benefits.

Display a respected opinion and create peer pressure to follow suit.

E-mail the URL to friends and acquaintances.

Advertise the product in their 'favorites' lists, blog, or by posting traditional banners.

They are advertisers though they are most often unaware of it and normally do not get paid for it. Yet they are much more effective than most expensive marketing campaigns because they are on the inside track. They are at the heart of things.

On social and word-of-mouth networks, people feel comfortable discussing their favorite products because they don't feel targeted or exploiter by companies. As far as they are concerned, they are empowered. In their minds, they are making their own choices as a consumer. They have the power. Because of this, they promote more whole-heartedly the products they feel passionately about.

Sounds great, doesn't it?

In the tradition of this book following a no-nonsense, actionable approach, I'll start with a list of viral marketing ideas for the independent musician.

Think Of Your CD As A Virus

That's right. Your CD is a virus. And there are roughly seven billion potential carriers of this virus. With more and more competition vying for the hearts and minds of the buying public, it's getting more and more difficult to penetrate the market. You need to find the people who are going to be good spreaders of your virus and pass it on with ease to others. This could be the media or it could be personal bloggers – people who use social networks. Treat them well and give out creative incentives liberally.

Every time your band name gets mentioned, or your CD gets reviewed, think of your virus getting stronger. The more of a push you give it, the stronger it gets and the more viral it becomes.

The people who will spread your virus the most are the people who others trust. Some of these people are the music authorities – the bloggers, the podcasters, the radio hosts, the reviewers. Let the music authorities spread your virus!

[83]

Ask yourself, "What can I do to make my product more like a virus?" Have you thought about the context of your music? Sure, your songs have intense meanings. How can you spread those meanings? Is there anything that would engage the general public? Relate to them? Aggravate them? Amuse them? Upset them? Inspire them to respond or share an opinion of their own?

What if you posted relevant videos all over the internet related to your songs – possibly something timely or controversial. Something political? Something hilarious? Be honest with yourself. If you stretch yourself and turn your image into a gimmick, people will know. Also, you may think that your political punk band has something to say and is connecting with people, but connection is energetic. You could be missing the mark completely, and this point is critical. Looking at your music and how it's connecting or not connecting with people could take some contemplation.

Try Taking Over One Location At A Time.

If you're going to war or playing RISK, you don't send small amounts of troops to every country and hope things turn out for the best. You build a strong base and spread it in a way that no one has the strength to beat you.

One way to try to go viral is to take over one location at a time. Pick a forum, a website, a social network, or hey, a country. Why not? Ever hear of artists getting big in Japan or Germany? It could work as a fun experiment, and has worked for many bands. Simply focus in particular on your country of choice on social networks. Look up the music websites and zines for that country and get involved. You'd be surprised.

Many countries have large populations eager to hear new and original music. You may find that the North American crowd can tend to be cynical and close-minded to your marketing at times. Focus on another country and let them spread your music and message! This translates and spreads elsewhere.

On a smaller level, if you choose a website and get a good review, obviously you have had conversations with and befriended the reviewer if you've followed the behind-the-scenes marketing strategy. Here are some other ways to dominate the website and community associated with it.

Use the leverage from your review to score an interview and also a featured band spot.

Send your news releases regularly so the website is consistently reporting on your band. Make sure it's relevant.

Send free digital or physical copies to the rest of the staff, thanking them for the support of your band.

Follow the publication on Facebook, Twitter, and Pinterest and support them consistently. They will notice.

Show up on the forums with your website in your signature.

Comment on their blogs and reviews. Be relevant and positive.

Reach Out To Their Readership When Possible.

Talk to people and encourage them to spread the virus. If you wanted to get popular in school you would find out who the cool kids are and befriend them. If you want to get popular on a social network, look up the top personal users. Contact them and introduce them to your music. Befriend them. Take an interest in them. Create reasons why they should spread your music. Use incentives when needed. Reward the people who are on your side.

Use What Works On You

When you scour a music website or magazine looking for a new band to add to your iPod playlist or CD collection, only a select few will stand out to you. Why is that? Is it their artwork? The promotional language used to describe the band? The reviews listed? Is it the band photo?

Rearrange your own press materials and advertising if necessary to emulate (within reason) what looks effective to you. You will be marketing to people who relate to you, remember.

Are You Ready To Make Your Product A Virus?

Make sure you've prepared the necessary elements to go viral. Your website, music and content must be intact and impressive. Your product must be interesting! Ask yourself objectively "Would I spread this around? Would I tell my friends about this?" If the honest answer is no, don't panic. This just means there is still room for more creativity and experimentation.

Use Your Current Allies.

Make a list of everyone who is on your side. Keep track of their names, roles (family, radio dj, blogger, fan, etc), and email addresses on a document such as Microsoft Excel or a custom program. Keep them in the loop at to what's new with your band and how they can help you. Make it worthwhile and treat them well. Whenever you get played by a new radio show or get covered by a new website, add them to your list of allies. Once again, use cross-promotion, incentives and thank yous to keep them on your allies list.

Multiply Your Allies

Yes indeed. Ask your current allies if they know anyone else you can contact for airplay or press. You may be surprised what comes up. Ask if you can tell this new person that you were referred by them. They will usually be delighted to give you a few names.

Plus, approaching someone new saying "John Smith highly recommended your radio show for our band and suggested that I get in touch with you. John recently interviewed us at his Rock Star Nation website. Would you be interested in a review or interview?" gives you a much better chance of getting coverage than approaching on your own. By helping you, they see themselves doing a favor or coming through for a friend. Their ego is stroked just by knowing that someone recommended them. Most people will want to come through in this type of scenario.

Make your marketing plan your own social network. Multiply your allies to build your army. Pretty soon you will have enough press to rival a major label act. It's all about image.

Randomly Reward People

Word-of-mouth is not always created by set-in-stone freebies and campaigns. What does this mean to you? Well, it's a very good idea to randomly reward people. Go above and beyond.

If a new person signs up for your street team, mailing list, or buys your CD, why not send them a personal email letting them know you've sent them digital copies of 2 of your albums to say thanks. Most people would be thrilled to be contacted personally by a member of the band, and on top of that be given free stuff, they would surely tell a few friends. Be generous on a person-to-person basis and you'll be surprised at the word-of-mouth this can generate about your band.

Psychological Appeal

Ask for advice. This may sound like a simplistic tip, but it's actually a highly effective way to create real movement in your path. Did you know that it's been scientifically proven that people are far more likely to want to help when they're asked for their advice? It's even better to ask for their expertise.

Why? We all love having our ego's appealed to. If we're just asked for help point blank, we may think "Why should I help this person?" There is no relationship building. However, simply foregoing the begging part and approaching an industry professional, no matter the level, and telling them your situation, then asking for their expertise or if there is anything they can recommend, can have lucrative results. They may send you to one of their contacts. They may take you under their wing. They may advise you on something you're doing wrong and help you with the next steps. Just be sure your request is concise and nothing close to a sob story!

Everything At The Same Time

If you're an independent artist you most likely have an issue with timing, and it's directly related to finances as well as the feeling of being overwhelmed. If this is the case, save up for longer before launching your product, because in order to even hope for direct competition with other artists, you need everything to happen at the same time; your album release, your tour, your music video launch. You need to be busy all the time.

This is especially effective when you've built up a huge contact list of allies who are loyal to you. Send them your new music video and press release along with a personalized message all at the same time. Dozens of blogs posting about you at the same time can really catch the attention of outsiders, and that's ultimately what you want. A post here and there can still have effect, but it's tough to build the momentum.

Do Not Worry About Profit Quite Yet

You've got to launch this thing in a big way before you focus specifically on profit. The CD orders will eventually become a positive by-product of your viral campaign. Be very generous. Create reasons for your band to have an inside circle. Does your website allow people to log in? Are there member benefits such as extra free downloads? Are you providing a good incentive for those fans who are signing up for your mailing list or E-team? When someone does buy your CD, are you giving them something else as well such as a digital copy of your previous album or a previously unreleased track?

If it's digital, it doesn't cost anything. One common mistake that independent bands and musicians make in this day and age is being overly stingy and paranoid about their music. Here's a tip: If your band records a CD, sets up a website with 30 second previews of each track and waits for the fans to come swooping in, it's simply not going to happen.

Bands spend a lot of time asking "Should we offer this track for free? Will that be too much? But we won't make any money!" This is the indie band's paranoia.

Remember that a digital product is infinite. When someone downloads your song, you have a new listener. Period. Yes, they may have downloaded it for free, but you have no less stock. Now that we are beyond dealing with physical products, you don't have to worry quite as much about running out of product and potentially giving away too much stock for promotional purposes.

Beyond that, you should actively be looking for potential virus carriers to send free music to! Tell them all you'd like in return is that they post it somewhere or send it to someone else. Tell them to treat your music as a virus. They will most likely get a kick out of the idea and be appreciative of your modern attitude. It's this attitude that is going to get your music spread. Don't waste time on the old school way of thinking – if you do that you may as well be a record label going out of business.

Another way to think of it is: The more places you are, the more places people can find you.

So it's simple. Get in more places! These days, it's not just the media that are turning people on to new music. It's the music fans, thanks to the help of social networking. Get your music into as many receptive hands as possible and encourage them to spread it themselves. Get into more places.

People Will Download Music For Free – No Matter What

You need to accept this. The record labels have not. Many artists have not. People will download music for free whether you offer your own music for free or not. Would you rather them have your music and potentially spread it or not? In fact, you not only need to accept the fact that people want free music. You need to embrace it and make it a core part of your promotional strategy.

The more music you have distributed for you free of charge, the more you will sell. Some of the people who catch the virus will be the ones who prefer to support the artist by paying for music. Just remember, right or wrong, it's the nature of the business today that music is essentially free. The only people who pay for music are those who:

Prefer to support the artist and have the funds to do so

Good Samaritans or people who feel it is wrong to download music for free

Do not have the means (such as a computer or file-sharing network) to download for free

[89]

Do not have the technical know-how to download for free

Sound blunt? Well, somebody's got to be honest! It's only when we stop beating our heads against the wall that we can try a new tactic. Smart bands can use both the paid and free methods if they so desire. Why not release a full-length for sale along with a free EP? More content is better, and this way you reach both markets.

Word of mouth has changed. This is an important thing to remember. Word of mouth has changed. And you can use this knowledge in your favor. Twenty years ago, if I loved a new band I would tell a few friends and maybe make a mix tape. Today, if someone gets into a new band, they may add the band name to their MySpace Music preferences, join the band's fan club on Facebook (typically all their friends will see this), add the band to their Last.fm playlist, mention the band in their favorite forum, and write about the band in their personal blog if they have one. Word of mouth is happening online in blogs, social media and forums. The bands who understand this are the ones that get known. A recommendation that would have died within a small friend circle previously now lasts forever on the internet. Use this to your advantage.

Don't underestimate the average Joe! It could be the biggest mistake you ever make. This is another reason to be generous with your music. The guy who you judged for nabbing your album without paying may be introducing your music to hundreds of new fans through a forum post or blog. Let it circulate and don't judge.

"Send This Page To A Friend"
On Every Page Of Your Website.

This is something that will put you ahead of the curve, and it's something very few independent musicians do. Give people multiple ways to spread your music around. This is one of the best ways. If bloggers do it, and news websites do it, why can't you? All it takes is an html code, and you can look these up quite easily using Google search. If someone really enjoys one of your songs or blogs, this gives them an opportunity to send the link to their friends immediately. Statistics show that these options work, and without them, people simply would not go to the effort in most cases to refer. You will need a free script to download to add this feature to your site.

Spread Your Music Through Banner Promotion

Make your banner and banner code available. Create an incentive (see a theme here?) for people to post it on their own websites. You could offer the first 10 people to add your banner (or song, for that matter!) to their website a free download. Once that's done, start a different contest. You should also have professional banners ready to go for advertising purposes.

In order to add a banner to your site that shows people a code they can easily post on their own websites, here is a template:

```
<br><br> <img src="YOUR IMAGE " border="0">
<br>COPY / PASTE<br>the code below to your site to link
to our band!<br><textarea name="textarea" cols="70" rows="3">
<a href="YOUR WEBSITE "><img src="YOUR IMAGE "
border="0" /></a><br /></textarea> <br><br>
```

Just copy the above code into your website and add in your details. This will allow people to spread the word for you by posting the banner themselves.

Create an E-Card

Have an E-Card created for your band. E-Cards are a perfect example of viral marketing. The idea is for people to forward them to each other. Start it off with your family if you have to! They're the most proud of you! They may have people on their email lists who will forward it on for you.

Send your music to podcasts and internet radio shows. I'll go over specifics about these later, but the spreading of your music to new listeners through these formats is a form of viral marketing.

Create a downloadable screensaver: Make a simple screensaver that has your website address and band name in bold letters. Design a particularly artistic screensaver and people will be more inclined to keep it. You can download simple to use software at www.download.com

Be controversial or compelling. We talked about this earlier. Remember the press release reference to the "Louisiana rock band slams Obama"? Well, how about posting a YouTube video with his photo? How about an e-card that people can spread virally? Only do this if it suits your music. No matter what your subject matter, there should be a viral market for you.

MUSIC VIDEO PROMOTION

Music video promotion is a topic that mystifies most independent artists, and it's for this reason that I decided to intensify my focus on this subject for this edition of "Your Band Is a Virus". It's easy to get caught up in the excitement of making a music video, which is something akin to an experience of show business for first-timers. Making a music video is something you should be excited about, but don't let it detract from the work that's ahead. Simply posting your video and hoping for support from your friends and fans is inexcusable, unless you just did it for fun.

There are professional music video distribution and promotion companies such as Hip Video Promo (www.hipvideopromo.com), Rive Video (www.rivevideo.com), and Trendsetter (www.trendsettermarketing.net). All of these companies have major artists as well as indies on their rosters. They basically prepare and format your video for television's sometimes stringent requirements, promote the final product to the MTV network, Fuse, BET, MuchMusic, Pitchfork TV, California Music Channel and a host of others, not to mention retail pools, clubs, video-on-demand and popular music video websites that tend to be somewhat inaccessible from the outside. Each company has different capabilities and it's important to do your own investigation. Pricing is typically similar to what you'd pay for a music promotion company to promote your album; often not as high as artists imagine.

I highly recommend that you put aside $3000 or more to promote your music video in various ways if possible. Don't solely rely on a music promotion company. However, for those who cannot afford to invest much money into their video, there are manual things you can do to maximize your exposure.

Get on YouTube

This should always be in the form of a professional video (It's not as difficult as you think. Hire a film student to shoot your video for you. It will cost a fraction of the price of a professional director and should produce some good results) or simply well-done footage of one of your live performances. Make sure it's of a high enough quality or it can actually work against you. Content is key, but good content is everything. These days there is no excuse for poor quality. Even iPhones have amazing video features that should allow you to put together an impressive HD live video.

You can show a slideshow of your band photos and post a song from your latest CD. It can be invaluable to become familiar with YouTube as an independent artist. Use stock footage, footage of political figures or current events, something artistic or eye-catching – anything that represents the mood of your music or will potentially get people talking, and more importantly, spreading your virus. You can use relevant keywords to attract people to your video. Many bands have gained thousands of new fans by simply posting a slideshow or video on YouTube. Is there a new movie coming out that has gained a lot of buzz? Post clips of the movie set to one of your best songs. As the recent Alice in Wonderland movie approached, many bands took this opportunity and set their own music to clips of the upcoming film. This resulted in thousands upon thousands of listens, and many new fans. Make sure to build those relationships as well. Comment other similar sounding bands and music outlets. Sign up for their channels and favorite their videos. Build your network.

Get Creative

If it's controversial or current in some way, that is even better. For example, there is a live video on YouTube of a performance by the Dillinger Escape Plan where the singer runs into the crowd frantically, stepping on their shoulders, screaming his head off, the whole bit. People started spreading this video virally and it helped spread the word about the band.

[94]

The point is, if people like your video and your music they will tell their friends about it. In lieu of having a professionally done music video, there are plenty of things you can do to gain thousands of new fans online.

To create your music videos from slideshows and video clips combined you can use free software programs like Windows Movie Maker, for example. If you want something more professional and you are ok with spending some money you can always try:

Adobe Premiere Elements 4.0

Power Director 6

Vegas Movie Studio 8

Set Up Your Own Channel On Youtube

Having your own channel is a great way of attracting people to your music, and for creating a thriving community. Within your YouTube channel you can add your favorite videos by others. When those videos are viewed, your channel is visible which means that YouTube users are able to click through and find out what else your channel has to offer. This is a perfect reason to expand your content.

Think about the kinds of things your fans love to watch and save them to your YouTube channel. It's a great way to bring people into contact with your music. In order to create more magnetism for your channel, try using a custom photo background. This emulates Youtube artist pages and gives you your own professional stamp.

Distribute Within Youtube

There are plenty of music curators who have YouTube channels, one of the most popular being www.Blanktv.com, a website that caters to rock, punk, alternative and metal music videos. They re-upload the artist's music videos to their own YouTube account, resulting in many more views for the artist as a result. The amount of channels on YouTube is quite extensive, and it would take some digging to find them, but a good start is searching terms such as "independent music", "Music videos", "unsigned", and also genre terms like "metal", "alternative", and "hip hop" while using the channel filter. The more you show up within YouTube, the more potential for your music to be bounced around and show up in search results.

Tag It Up And Optimize

Properly labeling and tagging your YouTube video is important. Since YouTube's search function is impartial, accuracy is more important than hype. Ideally, the video title, description, and tags should contain repeat words, with the band name appearing in all three. YouTube allows for quite a few comments, so be sure to include everything relevant to your video that people may search for, even similar bands that appear in your bio, for example. Also, make sure to include full website, sales page, and contact information in the info section, on top of including your full bio and band information.

Most bands skip this step, but a detailed description of your YouTube video is a big part of how people find you (not just on YouTube, but on Google as well), and how your video goes viral. Being thorough with your title, video information and tagging is called optimizing your meta-data.

Advertise

One idea that bands often disregard on YouTube is advertising partnerships. You can allow YouTube to show advertising at the beginning of your music videos and make money in the process.

In fact, YouTube recently launched a partner program specifically for indie bands. Bands who are accepted will get to add tour dates and "buy" links for music and merchandise and exert further control over the design of their pages. On top of this, their music will be much easier for new fans to find thanks to their new partnership with the ones controlling the search. See how that works? Start thinking like a business and outsource!

Advertise! You can apply for consideration at the following link: http://www.youtube.com/musicianswanted

Annotations

Annotations are also a great way to further promote your band/brand, generate more emails for your mailing list, more merchandise sales and more downloads of your latest album. They are small sections of text layered over the vide itself that allow you to input additional information such as download links, other videos or your channel subscription box. Think of this as free advertising.

Start Strong No Matter What

It's critical that you start strong when releasing a new music video on YouTube. Since it's much trickier competing for valuable tags later in the game, it's important that your video gets extensively viewed and rated. This is why many bands will use Fiverr gigs and other social media companies to boost their YouTube views. Be careful with these and do your research if you hire anyone. Make sure your promotions are always organic and not automated. This ensures that real people see your video, and also that you don't get unnecessarily banned.

Share Your Album

YouTube seems like an unlikely place to share your album, but in fact it's one of the best. It's a great idea to upload each track on your album along with the album cover as the image to YouTube. Many people use YouTube as their sole music discovery platform, and won't think you're relevant if you don't have much content available. This also gives you more chances to share your "Buy the album here" links.

Vimeo

Vimeo describes itself as "a respectful community of creative people who are passionate about sharing the videos they make. We provide the best tools and highest quality video in the universe." It's true – Vimeo has long been a hub for artists and video directors, and it's generally free of much of the low quality distractions that pollute YouTube's search results. Also, their moderators actively watch the comments for anything abusive or over-the-line, so the community remains generally free of excessive buffoonery.

Vimeo's channels and groups are quite easy to search for, and communicating with the users in charge is easy too. On top of this, Vimeo has member forums where you can get involved and cross-promote with others. Basic accounts allow up to 500MB of storage.

Metacafe

Metacafe.com is a video sharing website that surpasses 40 million visitors a month. That's some heavy traffic. This community is moderated, and all new videos are checked out by volunteers. They also have a focus on short videos clocking in at less than 10 minutes – perfect for the music video format.

Blip.TV

Blip.tv focus on original content and their audience is well worth reaching out to. They also offer a distribution service which will promote your video to YouTube, Flickr, Myspace, and AOL Video among others. They offer both free and pro accounts, but you need a pro account to use their special features.

Daily Motion

Dailymotion.com is similar to YouTube in the sense that it's not moderated and as such, allows just about everything.

Muzu.tv

Muzu.tv is an Irish website that features music videos from artists worldwide. This is a site where people actively seek out independent music videos. They have quite an active following and also pay artists 50% of ad revenue on their content. That's a novel idea.

[98]

Other Online Video Distribution Options

Sound daunting? Don't want to do all of that yourself? Luckily there are many options available for video distribution to online channels. Sites like www.videowildfire.com, www.tubemogul.com, www.veoh.com, and www.heyspread.com offer different options for distributing your music video to popular websites. Some have free options, but it's best to go with some sort of paid option in order to take advantage of the extra features. Heyspread.com allows you to purchase credits specifically for the sites you wish to reach. For example, if you only wanted to distribute to Vimeo, Facebook, Google, Yahoo and Daily Motion, that's all you would pay for.

Music Video Promotion Through Blogs

This is an obvious point, but…music blogs don't just review albums. In fact, they rarely review albums in comparison with other things. Whenever you visit just about any music blog, chances are you see more music videos than anything else. In fact, it would be a challenge to find a blog that didn't post music videos. For this reason, saying you don't know where to promote your music video is kind of like saying you can't find the internet.

People are more visually focused now than ever before. It's for this reason that a music video is not only critical to have, but it should be the leading part of your promotional strategy. Posting your music video embed code is much easier for a blogger than spending 2 hours writing an in-depth review of your album. Give bloggers the option. Most video views happen from blog exposure, not on YouTube.

The Channel Search

It's not as difficult as you might think to submit your own music video to popular online and television channels. Some require strange formats, and in those cases it's best to enlist the help of the pros, but some accept a simple Quicktime file on DVD and a signed contract, or even better, a .mov file. One of these examples is the hugely popular California Music Channel, which is open to independent artists of all genres and can be found at http://www.cmc-tv.com/submissions.htm. Aux.tv also accepts Quicktime files on DVD. Be sure to check their website for specific instructions. IndiMusic TV also allows independent music video submissions at

http://www.indimusictv.com/submitvideo.cfm.

Google search the proper terms and you'll be surprised at the amount of channels you'll find.

ABC's RAGE accepts independent artists. Details are available here: http://www.abc.net.au/rage/submissions/

http://videos.antville.org/ and www.iheartmusicvideos.com allow you to **post** links to music videos after setting up an account, and its well worth it considering their built in audience. I've had great results using both websites. Baeblemusic.com and BlankTV.com both accept music video submissions online. They only accept high quality; Baeblemusic accepts all genres and BlankTV sticks to rock of all kinds.

Here are some more websites that accept music video submissions. There are literally thousands of others, but I hope this will get a positive, frenzied thought process started for you.

www.roxwel.com

http://pitchfork.com/tv/

www.deadsinkonline.com

http://trendymusicvideos.com/submit

www.indie360magazine.com

www.bugvideos.co.uk

www.indiefeed.com

Want a bigger list? Check out:

http://www.ovguide.com/browse_sites?c=music&ci=407 for a listing of major and independent music video websites. You will need to do your own research to find more that suit your music, however.

If you have a stunning music video, why not enter it in some significant competitions such as the Independent Music Awards (www.independentmusicawards.com) or the International BBC Music Video Festival (http://bbcmusicvideofestival.tumblr.com/).

HOW TO EARN MORE FUNDS

A big question often asked in today's music market is how independent musicians can sell product. After all, most people steal their music these days, right? Well, not exactly. There are still ways to make money at this thing called music. We'll go over a wide range of tips.

Create abundance in your mind:

A lot of musicians have unhealthy attitudes towards money. Many musicians tell themselves that money is unimportant. If you want to be a successful musician, you will need to discard this idea right away. Call it "punk rock ethic". Call it whatever you like. If it doesn't help you, it's just a convenient world view – an excuse.

Change your attitude:

There is a lot of doom and gloom in musician's minds these days. Don't even hang around with these people, let alone allow yourself to be one. Music should be played for the love of itself before all else. Don't let anyone convince you that your art is not welcome in this world. Be a positive force.

Don't be daunted by your friends and family:

Your friends and family, in most cases, are going to be unsupportive. They'll tell you they love your music – just don't expect a CD sale. It's just the way things are. That's ok, because it's the outside world you want to reach anyway. Don't let it get you down. Put yourself in their shoes. Do you really want to go to your cousin's dance recital? Your art is for the world, not your family. It will save you endless discouragement if you just expect nothing from them. Believe in yourself and don't let it stop you.

[101]

Customize your content:

Not everyone wants the same old CD. Many artists are finding the secret to earning more money is targeting niche groups. Making custom merchandise for each tour stop is an idea that will engage your fans and also give them the feeling of individuality. Why would they want the same t-shirt that everyone else has? Hunter's caps and baseball caps, or possibly shot glasses, could end up being your biggest sellers, so don't write off any options.

Limited edition:

That sounds enticing, doesn't it? People are attracted to scarcity. Limited edition vinyl pressings or CD releases can generate amazing results. Some record labels even adopt this strategy, limiting each release to only 500 or 1,000 copies. This could even encourage pirating of your music, which, as I mentioned earlier, isn't a bad thing. It just means you're in demand. It's hard to create that demand when there are limitless amounts of the same product.

Target the market with buzz:

I wrote earlier about "creating the frontline". This may take a few months, but once it's complete, your band looks much more appealing to the buyer. Go to www.kyshera.com and check out their press section. This is a perfect example of impressive press quotes, and you can certainly take it further. In order for you to be in demand, and for your product to be in demand, you need to "appear to be" in demand. Get it? This is why it's so important to have 50, 60, 100, 200 reviews, blog posts, and press quotes. Fan-made videos and forum posts as well as news releases and an active fanbase spreading them all make a difference. Appearances become reality, especially when the buzz is warranted.

Get busy, look busy, and stay busy:

Some bands don't sell and they can't identify the problem. Maybe your album came out 6 months ago and you've been playing a show a month ever since. People can tell when you're not busy, and it's not all in relation to live shows. People can just sense when the momentum is missing. That's the best way I can explain it. This is why it's important to record multiple bonus tracks, even extra EP's, high quality live audio and live videos. If you're not releasing a new album for another year, it would be a huge benefit to put out something new monthly to appease your fanbase and encourage growth. As a result, the outside world will see your band as productive content providers, and worth following up on. The band that waits around loses.

Stream your music and don't believe the hype:
Many new streaming services have popped up over the past 10 years, and they have mainly been controversial because of their typically horrible payment rates. Spotify leads the pack here and is generally the most heavily criticized of the bunch. Pandora, Last.fm and Jango are other popular streaming sites. What many musicians don't understand when they debate on forums about these things is that these changes are most likely here to stay, and most importantly, a significant portion of people choose to discover their music through sites such as these. If you withhold your music because of political reasons, you miss out. Some people stream in order to decide what to buy, as well, so being accepted in the streaming game can mean more sales.

Go viral:
Get people posting your mp3's and sales links all over the place (the ones you want distributed, anyway). Persuade people to write about you in their blogs and forum posts. Put up YouTube videos featuring your songs. Spread the message far and wide.

Talk to people:
Be a real person. Talk to people on Facebook. Comment their profiles. Participate on forum chats. ALWAYS leave your web address as your signature. Many people are more likely to buy your CD if they feel they have had a good conversation with

[103]

you or that they 'know someone in the band'. It's a win-win situation.

Solve a problem:
Who needs your music? There are niches out there that your music can fill. Is your music good for meditation? Could it be used by a political activist organization? Could it be marketed to others who are in line with your beliefs? How could it be useful in people's actual daily living?

Covers:
Everyone knows that cover bands make way more money than original acts. The covers market is lucrative and shows no signs of letting up. Sure, you may want to wear a mask to hide your real identity, but gigging regularly as a cover band could earn the funds you need to properly promote your original band. Just saying!

Note: Only you know if this is a good option for your band. I don't typically recommend it as I personally prefer bands who are uncompromising. However, anything that allows a band to save up if a positive thing; even if it's children's parties.

Play live:
I constantly hear artists saying that "if a good live opportunity comes up, we'll do it". I'll save you some time in telling you that if you're waiting for someone to knock on your door and bring you out on tour, you're going to be waiting a long time. It's important for many reasons that you play live and play often. All the tactics in this book should help you, but it's arguable that the single most important thing for you to do is to play live. Book your own tour or hire a booking agent. Don't whine about the fact that you have a job. You're the captain of the ship. You're just contradicting yourself, which brings me to my next point.

Mixed signals:
Most bands fail to create momentum and really sell/create

demand because they send mixed signals. They say they want to be in Rolling Stone and travel the world but expect someone to do it for them. The world is always against them somehow, and it's easy to see through.

This isn't even something that should be said when it comes down to it. It puts a jam in the works, doesn't it? The main thing to understand is this. All of us human beings, we are all in the same situation more or less. We all experience the same sorrow. We all go through hardship. Most of us don't have what we need to live a healthy life. Most of us are poor.

No one cares about your particular situation. It's neither unique nor special in any way. It doesn't even matter how justifiable your story is. Whether you broke your leg or you got a disease, there's a point when complaining loses its potency. Complaining about Spotify, Sonicbids, or entertainment lawyers won't do any good. Don't let being in a band be your thing to complain about. Do your research and set an example by showing a positive face to the world.

Music consultants will tell you that at the independent level, bands and band members must be accessible. So create profiles for each of your band members and make them accessible. Provide contact information for each member on your official website. Add their individual profile information to your Twitter account. Some people may have questions for the lyricist about the meaning of a particular song. Other people may want to ask the guitarist about his gear, or how he or she got started. Once they get that friendly response directly from the member of the band it will get them on board. They will be a loyal fan and much more likely to buy a CD.

Steal your way to the top:
One of the best ways to get ahead is to steal tactics. Find bands that are similar to yours but more successful. What are they doing right? Start connecting with their fans. Connect with them and ask their advice. Post comments on their page – the less spammy and the more personal, the better.

[105]

SOCIAL NETWORKING, FILE STORAGE, AND OPPORTUNITY WEBSITES

As an independent musician, you should create a presence on as many of these websites as possible. We discussed Facebook, Twitter, Bandcamp, Soundcloud, Last.fm and Reverbnation in detail earlier. Here are some other sites you can utilize to promote and store your music. Use all of their tools to your advantage:

Music XRay –Music XRay allows independent musicians to submit their music for potential licensing in film, television, video games, label roster consideration, radio play, or for review in magazines and blogs.

Musicclout.com – An opportunities website for musicians with a truly fresh face and approach. Unlike many others, they are genuinely plugged in. I've worked with them directly, and they take a personalized, friendly approach and are also music lovers themselves. I also have a good impression of them because their artist quality is high. Artists can submit their music for record label A&R, management, magazine review, music festival, licensing deal and touring consideration amongst other things.

Dropbox.com – Dropbox is fast becoming very popular amongst musicians and music bloggers alike. Some blogs list it as their preferred method of receiving music and files from artists.

Mediafire.com – Mediafire is another common file storage website used by a majority of bloggers and musicians. It's perfect for your album zip file.

MySpace.com – It once was the ultimate social network for musicians, and now only a shadow of its former self. In today's music market many are suggesting that bands do away with the MySpace profile and stick to Bandcamp, Soundcloud, Reverbnation, Facebook, Twitter and an official website. However, it's good to properly set up your profile. Just don't spend much time on it.

Flickr.com – Flickr is a very popular photo sharing social network. Post photos of your fans, the audience at your shows, your tour photos, you at music festivals. Get your fans involved in your band through your photography. This site can become a very effective marketing tool. The search results on Flickr are different and much more extensive in many cases than Google. Encourage your fans to send photos of the band (or themselves at one of your shows) to add to your Flickr page.

Google Reader (www.google.com/reader) -- RSS feed aggregator (Learn about RSS. It could become the most important aspect of your website.)

Tumblr.com – scrapbook blogs, or 'tumblelogs'. Many bands are taking advantage of the fast-rising popularity of the Tumblr community.

Wikipedia.org - all of human knowledge in editable form. Add your information only when relevant. If you are a young band, keep the item to the point. Include links to online articles referencing you so the information can be easily verified. Do not add yourself until you have set up a strong presence, have played live extensively, and have garnered a high amount of press and reviews. Wikipedia tends to delete bands who they consider to be irrelevant.

www.Del.icio.us - social book marking

Bloglines.com - RSS feed aggregator

Dropcash.com - make your own fundraiser

Feedburner.com - customize and enhance your feed

YouSendIt.com - send big files without clogging email (Ideal for sending digital copies of your album to potential reviewers. Get familiar.) If you end up choosing Bandzoogle as your website host, they also have a feature which allows you to send digital albums free of charge.

Wordpress.com - blogging platform

Imeem.com - social networking site, like YouTube, though you can stream music and photos as well. Merge your music, videos and photos in order to gain new fans. Your playlists can be rated by others and ranked, which is a definite plus. The top rating playlists on Imeem receive over 2 million plays.

Jumpcut.com - online video editing and remixing

Reddit.com - popular links shared and commented

Dropload.com - send big files

Diigo.com - social bookmarking and annotation

Vox.com - social networking through blogging

Mog.com - music sharing through blogging

Artistdata.com - Artist Data could turn out to be a highly valuable timesaver for you. Upload your details to Artist Data and have them sent all over the place – for example, to MySpace, Last.fm, etc. Keep your news distributed and your fans up to date.

MORE STRATEGIES

Blog comments: Comment on other people's blogs. Make sure you include your band's web address so people can check you out. Keep in mind your comments must be relevant to the blog and not for spamming purposes. If your comments are interesting, people are more likely to visit your website.

Email signatures: Make sure every email you send has a signature with your website on it. This is another way to build your profile. For example:

James Marsdon

The Dead Animals – Goth Rock Band from California

www.thedeadanimalsrock.com

jamesmarsdon@thedeadanimalsrock.com

(Insert phone number here as well as relevant social media profiles here)

Posting in forums: Careful with this one! Don't bother setting up fake profiles and answering your own posts about your music. The administrators, and in most cases everyone else, will be able to tell you are doing this and it could ruin your reputation. To participate in forums, follow the blog commenting procedure. Make your posts relevant. Get into conversations about topics you care about. Get people to respect your opinion. And of course, include your website as your signature in every post. People will check you out.

Outsource everything: Why not get as many people promoting you as possible? Use micro-job websites such as Fiverr.com to hire people to do everything from write a review to dancing around on a YouTube video while carrying a sign with your band name!

Unique content as a sales pitch: Pitch yourself as a perfect interview subject to as many blogs as possible. Use the term "unique content" in your request. Blogs go crazy over this because it translates to relevant content for their blog with very little effort required on their part. Not many bands promote themselves in this way and it just may help you get on some bigger blogs outside of your main niche.

Don't stick with music: Another issue that musicians come across when bombarding music blogs requesting coverage is the intensive competition. Many of these publications get hundreds to thousands of emails a day, so it's best to think outside of the box. Many publications have music sections, but get far less music requests than their music blog cousins. Some of these publications have massive followings; entertainment, lifestyle, sports, men's, women's, tattoo, political, spiritual, regional. There are endless niches you could be targeting that you probably haven't thought of yet. Go where the other bands are not and drink the fine wines!

PODCASTS

Podcasting today is pretty much what radio used to be: shows about various topics that anyone can put together, upload as an MP3, and broadcast to the public through RSS. There are all types of podcasts and they differ wildly in size of audience - some with only a few listeners, others with tens of thousands. With podcasting, music and video content is available by subscription download. Once downloaded, it can be viewed or heard at the user's convenience. Users typically use software such as iTunes to subscribe and download the content.

Once downloaded, the files are ready to be listened to.

Getting your music on any podcast is one of the easiest ways to expose your music to potential new fans. In fact, getting played on podcasts could be lucrative to the success or failure of your online promotion campaign. Want to make this actionable and get started right away? Here's how.

Register your music with a podsafe collective:
Podcasters have set up podsafe music collectives to ensure the music they play is podsafe. This saves them from lawsuits and legal hassles from both artists and record labels. To get on the list, these podsafe music collectives ask musicians to sign up and upload songs that are safe for podcasters to play. By registering and uploading songs, you agree to make your music podsafe under a podsafe license. Some of these collectives include the Podsafe Music Network (http://music.podshow.com) and Podsafe Audio (www.podsafeaudio.com). Podsafe Audio uses a Creative Commons license. One thing that differentiates many podcasters with the average radio DJ is that podcasters are often eager to hear your music. They do not get paid for what they do and they do it out of a love for music. They tend to appreciate it when artists send their music. Remember, they are independent too, so be personal and get them on your side. Being on the playlist for

[111]

relevant podcasts can be extremely helpful to getting your band known.

Choose podcasts that are relevant to your style:

If you are a groove rock band, don't bother the jazz podcast asking them to check out your music. But do contact any and all podcasts who play your genre. Use the same tactics we talked about in our Behind-the-scenes marketing chapter.

Promote them in return:

Podcasts love cross-promotion. They want more listeners, just like you do. It's a match made in heaven, so no need for all the promotional language. Talk to them like human beings and offer to help however you can in return for them playing your music.

Create your own podcast:

Another option for you independent musicians is to create your own podcast. It doesn't have to be a simple playlist of your music. You can include a band interview, describe the meaning being your song, show your sense of humour, lash out with your best political rant or announce a contest.

It's easy to do. Here's what you will need:
• A computer
• An MP3 file to podcast
• Music editing/recording software
• Text-editing software
• An RSS text file
• Somewhere online to post your files

Let's assume you already have an original song saved as an MP3 file on your computer. You'll then want to add a voice-over track to complete the show. With free audio software like Audacity, you can quickly record and edit voice-over elements right on your computer. If you have any kind of home studio, you can easily create a higher quality recording.

Once compiled and edited, save the new file as an MP3. To make your file ready to podcast, there is specific ID and naming protocol you must follow. Yahoo has a helpful tutorial:
http://podcasts.yahoo.com/publish/1
Here's another well-done explanation.
http://www.podcastingnews.com/articles/How-to-Podcast.html.
You will then need to FTP your file to your own website, or use a hosting service like Host Gator.

One major benefit of podcasting regularly is that subscribers will automatically get updates whenever you post new episodes. To do this, you have to create an RSS feed for your podcast. The RSS feed alerts subscribers about your updated podcast and allows them to be downloaded immediately.

FILM AND TV PLACEMENT

Getting your music into a film or television show is great publicity. You can try to search for these opportunities independently or alternatively, you can sign up for one of many website services that connect independent musicians with independent filmmakers. Here are a few to check out and decide for yourself. Most of them have minimal membership fees. Research and try them out and see what works for you.

www.musicdealers.com
www.taxi.com
www.pumpaudio.com
www.audiosocket.com
www.rumblefish.com
www.youlicense.com
www.soundtraxservices.com
www.magnatune.com/info/submit
www.musync.com/about/
www.westwoodmusicgroup.com
www.nomamusic.com
www.beatpick.com
www.filmmusic.net
shootingpeople.org

GUERRILLA MARKETING
(Contacting Bigger Media and playing by the rules better than anyone else.)

How will the big guns notice you? Contacting larger media outlets can be trickier, and there are some cases where you will definitely want to follow the strict submission procedures. We're not backing off our "Behind-the-scenes marketing strategy" by any means! We're just saying people who write for Rolling Stone tend to be less accessible. So if you are by chance submitting a news tip or asking for coverage by emailing editors@rollingstone.com (their actual news tip email), then you'll want to follow a few guidelines.

For the message title, all capitals is a no-no. "Next big thing" is also a no-no. It's common sense really. Think of what you would typically delete in your own inbox and don't send those types of titles!

A perfectly suitable title would go something like "New Stoner Rock Band from California". This way they know exactly what the message is about and it's not belligerent.

In the body of the message, address them by name whenever you can.

Be polite. They will appreciate it.

Introduce your act and get right to the point.

Check your grammar.

Your first email to a bigger media outlet should be more of a request than a full-blown release.

Keep it short. If they want more information, they will ask for it.

Include links and contact information for them to investigate.

Don't email mp3's straight away. Wait until they request it back from you. Even better than this is to include a secure link that contains all your media. Set yourself up with Dropbox or Mediafire, and put everything in clean zip files. Blogs should be able to get your new album, press photos, bio and music video within one or two clicks.

Follow up ONCE. Do this anywhere from five business days to two weeks after sending the initial email.

Become an easy target:

You need to be easily reachable. This does not just mean your Contact section on your website. Make sure you include your contact information on everything you send out, including your emails, newsletters and press releases. You don't want to miss the call because your phone number wasn't provided.

Niche yourself:

Don't you hate it when you ask someone what kind of music they listen to and they reply "Everything?" This usually means they are not passionate about ANY music, but are happy with whatever comes along on the radio. Are these people interesting? Would you want to get into a deep discussion about the meaning behind Pink Floyd's "The Wall" with one of these people? No!

Don't be that band.

Describe yourself!

Carve your niche and carve it well!

Say what you sound like! Use your influences if you like. Be proud of it.

Old school off-line promotion:
1. Have a hook.

Just like your favorite Smashing Pumpkins track has a killer chorus hook, your band's story needs to have a hook.

A hook must get people's attention right away. One sentence instead of twenty.

"Los Angeles rock band eats live goat on stage"

"Anarchism is alive and well and it lives in Seattle"

"London rockers dislike Nickelback, release new CD"

Those are extreme examples but we can guarantee you would at least check out the live goat one!

[116]

2. Don't give up.

You are the salesperson, the marketer for your band, so you must know what you're selling inside and out, and you must also know your customers (radio, media, etc). Respect what they need from you and follow through on it.

Be persistent. Call back. Follow up. And do it all in a personable way that gets them on your side.

3. Be honest.

People aren't stupid. It will help you in the long run if you are honest and upfront with everyone. Back up your claims.

PERFORMING RIGHTS ORGANIZATIONS

Performing rights organizations like BMI and ASCAP in America and SOCAN in Canada make it their job to collect on money owed to musicians from all revenue sources (TV, film, radio, live performances, and internet airplay such as podcasts).

When someone uses a song or piece you wrote, you are supposed to get paid. If it's a great opportunity, occasionally you can sign up for cross-promotion purposes, but make sure you get something out of it! Performing rights organizations gather up these monies, take a fee for doing so, and send you checks. If you make enough connections, you can eventually base a good portion of your income on this.

You have to register with one of the organizations to get this money. It's free to register and you can do it online, but you can only join one, not all. The two major organizations in the United States are:

BMI: www.bmi.com

ASCAP: www.ascap.com

Check them out and decide which one to sign up for.

Cue Sheets:

In order to get paid for having your music used in a film, the filmmaker has to turn in "cue sheets" to ASCAP and BMI. Cue sheets list the name of the movie, the name of the songs used, how many seconds of the song were used, at what point they are used in the film, the composer, and the composer's affiliation (ASCAP or BMI) and the name of their publishing company. (If you don't have a publishing company, you can make up your own company name when you join, and that is your publishing company. If you are your own publisher, you should join both as a composer and a publisher, and list both when you turn in info for cue sheets.

On a major company's production, they will definitely turn in cue sheets. On an independent film, you may have to get in touch with the producer or director and make sure he turns one in. You can even turn them in yourself.

For ASCAP's tutorial on Cue Sheets go to:
http://www.ascap.com/playback/2005/winter/cuesheets.html

For BMI's guide go to www.bmi.com
http://www.bmi.com/library/brochures/cuesheet.asp

BRANDING

Many bands and musicians try to hide themselves behind an air of mystique when representing themselves or promoting online. Artistically, a lot of artists try to follow the example of cryptic bands like Tool or Radiohead when promoting. This can work if you come up with the perfect marketing campaign, but normally it isolates you or produces the opposite effect of what you're looking for. Instead of appearing mysterious and larger-than-life, people view you as pretentious and difficult to relate to. The reason some bigger bands can get away with it is anticipation created by millions of dollars worth of promotion and years of building their brand. Some bands waste time on forums under fake aliases, hiding their identities in fear that it would ruin everything if they revealed themselves. This creates a lack of trust and it never really helps much.

So how can you, as an independent musician, create trust and build YOUR brand?

Reveal your identity:

The bands that stand out these days are the ones that show themselves to their fan bases. This means you have an online presence under your own name. It means you are accessible for your fans to talk to. It means you build an online presence for yourself. It means you are honest and open. Be confident. Stand behind your message. What do you have to hide?

Work from the gutter, on the frontlines, money or no money.

Use often-overlooked techniques to give your music wider exposure.

Build a following one fan at a time.

Celebrate each small success and USE IT. Use each success to gain you another one, to move forward.

Exploit your story. Get it out there. Be extreme and different.

Give stuff away. Don't expect anything if you're stingy.

Create Podcast & Radio ID's and Intros:

This is something that most bands don't do, and it costs them a lot of airplay. Independent radio shows and podcasts are always looking for bands to record custom song intro's and radio ID's to promote their show. An example of this is "Hi, this is James from Vancouver rock band The Slimy Snails and you're listening to the Non Stop Rock Podcast!"

When you initially contact the show, why not offer to record an ID for them? They will be 50 percent more likely to play your band, and much more keen on supporting you in the future.

Putting in this effort shows them that:

You took the time to listen to their show. You show that you're a real person.

B) You are taking the time to help the podcaster or radio host promote themselves. It shows them you're not just in it to get yourself out there. You want to return the favor.

Give Away Free Stuff:

This deserves its own section, as it's important for the spreading of your product. Websites (in relevant genres), music blogs, magazines, podcasts and internet radio appreciate nothing more than receiving product. This can be in the form of CD's, T-shirts, stickers, or any other products you want to throw in the package.

Yes, this will cost you some shipping fees, but it is critical that you invest in it. Each website that advertises your "Contest giveaway", first of all, becomes a dependable ally for you. Sending them product makes them much more likely to post features on your band, as well as the latest news.

The posting of the contest alone spreads the word about your band. The public perception of contests like these is normally associated with bigger bands, so it looks very good!

And of course the winners of these contests and everyone who checks out your website in the meantime, become new fans from all over the world.

So, don't sweat the cash. Once your album shipment is in, make sure you send multiple copies to all the hundreds of valuable allies you've gained through using the steps contained in our guide. Being generous and treating your "family" well pays off in spades.

Research your genre (and sub-genres):

This topic isn't discussed too extensively in other books. Unless you are one of those delusional bands who think they are a "space rock/jazz/funk/death metal/fusion/pop/contemporary hybrid", you most likely have a few genres you could be listed under. The reason we mention sub-genres is because they are absolutely valid. Many rock bands, for example, may have tracks that could be played in rock, indie rock, alternative rock, metal, industrial, progressive and hardcore formats. This may be a stretch for bands that have the same sound all the way through their respective albums, but you get the idea. The more genres you embrace, the wider your potential audience.

It's also important to research your potential media audience, because it's a big world out there and it's not all about Billboard Magazine.

There are specialty independent publications for everything from noise rock to eclectic progressive fantasy metal. They are putting their time into it for the love of the music, so get in touch with them. If you personalize it, you have a good shot. This is the way to build up your press section. It's all real people.

Another bonus: Guess who reads these strange music blogs and independent publications who cater to niche audiences? Well, you guessed it. Niche audiences. People who are fanatical about their music and trust the sources they get their information from. Get IN with these people. Befriend them and treat them well.

CROWD FUNDING

Many artists rejoiced when they found out about a fairly recent development in the online music world; crowd funding. Websites such as Kickstarter.com, Indiegogo.com and Pledgemusic.com allow artists, business owners, film directors, inventors, and fundraisers of just about every persuasion to set up a profile for their project and reach out for financial support from the public. Sounds simple, right?

This is where most people get tripped up. The most important thing to know about online crowd funding is that is functions exactly the same as raising funds in the physical world. You need to work at it...and hard. Artists should spend at least 40 hours promoting their crowd funding project and treat it like a job. If you want to reach the public, put the time and effort in.

One of the reasons that crowd funding can work so well is that it allows people to provide funding for your project in small amounts, and get value in return through the incentives you offer. While someone buying your CD through your website may suspect the funds could be going towards the drummer's next video game purchase, there is a real sense (and guarantee) that funds invested in a crowd funding campaign really go towards their progress, whether that be their new album, video, or tour.

Another aspect of the project campaign is the video. These need to be honest and original, giving a strong sense of who you are and what you're aiming to do with the album. When it comes down to it, what's the point of it? Why should they support you?

Only a small percentage of people who contribute to your campaign will do so solely to support you, so you'd better have amazing and creative incentives. Here are a few ideas:

The product – This is an obvious one. If someone contributes $10, they get a copy of your upcoming CD along with a personalized thank you note from the band.

The enhanced product – Why not create a deluxe version of the album only available to supporters of the crowd funding project? Throw in an extra disc of b-sides, live tracks and demo versions. If it gets bootlegged, don't worry. That's just more exposure and cool factor for you.

Start low – Amanda Palmer set a Kickstarter record by having 4,743 pledge for her $1 reward. What was the incentive? A digital download of the new album. With so many unknown artists being more concerned with getting their $9 through digital sales, this should provide some smart business perspective. One dollar can go a long way, both in supporting your project and gaining new fans.

Personalized material – Many artists do this and it seems to generate good results. When someone pledges $100 or more, why not write a song for them and perform it on Youtube? Granted, this is not the best choice for every band. It depends on your personality.

Cover tunes – If you want to stay within your image as a band, why not provide a list of covers for the public to choose from, and for a chosen bid, you record that cover and dedicate it to the bidder? This also gets more viral content on the net for your band, so it's a great tactic to use multiple times.

Rare merchandise – Why not appeal to your fanbase advertising merchandise only available through your crowd funding campaign? Limited edition t-shirts. Posters. Baseball caps.

Early access – Offer to send early demos and other exclusive content. This isn't just to wet people's beaks. It makes them feel as if they're genuinely a part of the making of the album, which they are.

Private parties – Why not arrange a private party and special performance specifically for supporters of your campaign?

Autographs – They're always popular. Sign CD's as well as endless photos.

Your back catalogue – Provide your full back catalogue as an added incentive for those who want more swag.

Something unusual – The really original ideas are going to be what sell your project. Fancy giving pledgers a remote reiki healing session, writing them a haiku, or sketching a cartoon?

For an example of a musician who succeeded in his Pledgemusic.com campaign and really did things right with his incentives, check out Jesse Terry's campaign'

http://www.pledgemusic.com/projects/jesseterry
For more ideas and tips, visit
http://www.kickstarter.com/blog/.

SONICBIDS WINNERS

Profiles on Independent Artists:

Last year I held a contest through Sonicbids.com, vowing to choose 5 independent artists who impressed me with their music, determination, and promotion tactics. I ended up choosing 7, and they are profiled below. I encourage you to follow these artists. Get in touch with them. Learn from them. Enjoy their music.

"ROOFTOP REVOLUTIONARIES"

Rooftop Revolutionaries are a hard rock trio from Los Angeles, California, who initially caught my attention with their explosive and very convincing track "I Am A War". The music is generally groove-driven and inspired by acts such as Rage against the Machine, but the vocals set the band apart with their unusually stellar melodic skill. It's unfortunate that there hasn't been new material from this act for some time now, as I'd love to see their next turn. Whether it be incorporating samples and electronics, or embracing the rock and roll end of the spectrum, I trust that their ship will not go astray for a few reasons.

One thing present in Rooftop Revolutionaries and their promotions is a message. While some bands scoff at the idea of having a message in your music, I think that's unfortunate. After all, there are only so many boy/girl scenarios artists can explore without sounding utterly mundane. Seeing a band like Rooftop Revolutionaries back up their politically charged lyrics with regularly updated opinion blogs, magazine and podcast interviews, and fan updates via their Facebook page shows consistency and care.

This band really has the potential to create a ton of organic word-of-mouth if they embrace the fact that their vocalist, Eleanor Goldfield, has some serious Janis Joplin machismo and melodic force, and the band are masters of heavy groove rock.

[126]

With these aspects combined, they have much more potential to fuse the spirit of freedom expressed in 60's acts like Jimi Hendrix and the Doors with modern rebel rock like Kyuss and Rage Against the Machine.

Find out more about Rooftop Revolutionaries and support their cause at:

www.rooftoprevolutionaries.com
www.facebook.com/rooftoprevolutionaries.

"DREAMKILLER"

Dreamkiller are a 4-piece heavy alternative/progressive band from Greensboro, North Carolina, who sum up everything that an independent band should be doing, and that's everything! When I first came across them in 2011, they already had an extremely impressive resume, and looking at how far they've come since I last touched base with them, it becomes an arduous task to even touch on their progress in a single article.

Their music itself is incredibly professional, but it's the sincerity behind it that makes it work as a whole. Far from a band trying to make it for the sake of success alone, vocalist Christy Johnson leads the charge with a very human and dynamic voice that communicates sincere, emotionally charged lyrics filtered through her sense of individualism. The music ranges from metal and alternative to punk-infused grooves, all uniting tastefully and supporting the songs.

If you want to model yourself after an artist's work ethic, learn about Dreamkiller. They are acting. They don't try their hand at a few opportunities and wait for them to come through. They keep going, and they push their music all the time, once again with Christy taking care of the promotional side of things. As a result, they won "Best Rock Band" at the very influential Independent Music Awards in 2011, as well as taking multiple LA Music Awards and Queen City Awards. Their music has been featured in over 10 films, so you can bet they are consistently active in seeking licensing for their music. They've also played Warped Tour, and now are building on their previous successes, landing a spot on the Xtreme Reverb Headliners National Tour 2013.

Dreamkiller is proof that when you start with a solid product, a unique perspective, and you take the business side seriously, you can go far by capitalizing on each success. Find out more about Dreamkiller at:

www.dreamkill.coma

www.facebook.com/dreamkillermusic.

"WILLIE AMES"

Some solo artists play the "woe is me" card, claiming that the odds are stacked against them because they don't have a band to share expenses and responsibilities with. I consider Willie Ames to be the exception to the rule, and a definite anti-thesis to the above character. He approaches his music, the music industry as a whole, and life it seems, with a positive and appreciative attitude. I was lucky enough to work with him to generate reviews for his brilliant "Night Owl" album, and the responses were all positive.

His work falls on the observant and wise end of the folk/acoustic singer songwriter spectrum. He takes influence from the likes of Bob Dylan and Fleetwood Mac, while adding his own unique spirit to the music.

Willies Ames has toured all 50 states and is currently in the midst of a 2nd U.S. tour as I write this. He doesn't have a tour booking company or a manager. He arranges all the shows himself. If that weren't enough, he personally distributes CD's to everyone in attendance at all of his shows. To date he has distributed over 35,000 CD's directly to fans. Now that takes some saving up. He's also won several awards, including "Solo Artist of the Year" at the 2010 LA Music Awards, "Best Male Performer" at the 2011 eMusic Awards, and "National Solo Artist of the Year" at the 2011 Phoenix Music Awards.

One of the core reasons why Willie Ames's music is catching on is because of his sheer will and determination. Many artists tend to get discouraged after cultivating a very harmful "all

or nothing" approach to their musical paths. Willie walks the path no matter what, and he reaches new fans every day because he refuses to put music on the backburner or get discouraged. The other core reason, of course, is the uniqueness and quality of the work itself. Find out more about Willie Ames at
www.willieames.com and www.facebook.com/willie.ames.

"SHOOT THE MESSENGER"

Shoot the Messenger is Rob Frail, a New York-based singer/songwriter who effortlessly genre-hops, embracing the eccentric and the poetic with his Talking Heads and Bob Dylan inspired musical and lyrical approach. His work is as intriguing as his voice is dynamic.

The world seems to generally agree with my assessment of this seasoned songwriter, who I'd go as far as to say has mastered his unique craft. 11 of his songs have won over 20 awards, including four notable honourable mentions at the Billboard World Song Contest. While many artists make themselves too coachable, willing to mold themselves to fit anyone's suggestion, Rob goes his own way, choosing to write material with actual meaning. Much of his work is socially conscious, even confrontational. In my humble view, the world would be richer if more artists actually spoke their truths rather than try to appeal to someone else's truth.

This is what makes Shoot the Messenger so appealing, and it's this uncompromising intensity that has gained him spots at a series of music festivals as well as several top New York City venues. To find out more about Shoot the Messenger visit
www.shootthemessengermusic.com
www.facebook.com/ShootTheMessengerMusic.

"TWELVE TWENTY FOUR"

Twelve Twenty Four are not your average rock band. Describing themselves as a "high energy, full-scale, holiday rock orchestra", this group of 17 talented individuals (and 8 person crew) manage to do something extremely difficult. They take

[129]

holiday favourites and amp them up in such a way that they become impressive, even inspiring, to Scrooge himself. I never listen to holiday music myself (except Boney M once in a while), and yet I can wholeheartedly admit that I would repeatedly play Twelve Twenty Four's "Miracle on Rock Street".

Part of the success of their formula is in having an idea that is unique and that appeal to a popular niche, one that can be targeted relatively easily. Beyond these aspects, the music is approached with a virtuoso flair inspired by acts such as Dream Theater and the Trans-Siberian Orchestra. The enthusiasm put into both the musical and live aspects makes them a magnet for new listeners and word-of-mouth. When people become this enthused, they genuinely want to help the band by spreading their message.

I predict that Twelve Twenty Four will continue to reach the masses, especially if they target their next well-produced release towards licensing for holiday themed films and fund the band through the proceeds. It could be a very lucrative holiday season indeed! Find out more about Twelve Twenty Four at

www.twelvetwentyfour.net
www.facebook.com/twelvetwentyfour.

"KEITH MOODY"

Keith Moody is the everyman...just not the everyman who sits on the couch watching his life go by. You can be certain of that! His music is classic rock with blues and country appeal, and he's certainly a refreshingly honest, raw voice in a genre that all too often relies on heavy commercialism. His achievements are far too many to mention, the result of his accessible sound and seemingly instant credibility from the listener's point of view.

He has received heavy radio play as well as licensing spots on the MTV network. His videos have been played on many major and independent music programs. He tours practically non-stop and he's landed endorsements with companies such as PRS Guitars and Elixir Strings. There isn't an aspect of the business that Keith hasn't researched and secured a strong foothold in.

While setting out on a journey such as Keith's, there would have been many challenges along the way, but as the accolades pile up into such an undeniable mountain, things get easier. Any industry person who glances at his Soncibids profile would see him as a definite choice, because he stays busy, and he's achieved more than most of his competition.

To find out more about Keith Moody:
www.keithmoody.com and www.keithmoodymusic.com.

"ORANGE GROVE"

Never underestimate what a truly universal message can do. Straight out of the Netherlands, Orange Grove is a 5-piece group who seamlessly mix positive lyrics with truly feel-good reggae and rock grooves. The earnest approach to their work on tracks such as "You Decide It" makes them instantly likeable and easy to relate to. You could call them "conscious reggae rock", for lack of a better term. Determined to put their all into the music and then show respect to that process by promoting heavily, Orange Grove have released 3 albums to date as well as multiple music videos. They extensively tour and have had their music licensed in various films and documentaries.

Much like Willie Ames, Orange Grove press forward and never look back. They continually look for opportunities in all aspects of the music industry, and it pays off. It also helps their cause that the positive energy put into their music results in that "special something" being expressed, and they're that rare band that you really want to rally for. I expect big things for them as they prepare to release new material, as well as team up with the highly anticipated "Children of the Wind" documentary, where several of their tracks will be featured.

Find out more about Orange Grove
www.facebook.com/orangegrove.

GET YOUR MUSIC HEARD THROUGH ONLINE CONTESTS

Guest Article by Jason Garriotte
Musician
www.chordsoftruth.com

Remix Contest:

The first type of contest we are going to cover is the Remix Contest. This will not only put your music in front of an audience of interested music producers, but will also generate new versions of your songs that will appeal to a completely different audience than your original recordings could ever reach. In fact, I had more plays and downloads within the first week of launching a remix contest than the previous 4 months since the release of my first album.

To give your contest the greatest chance of success it is important to provide everything that the remix producers need. While setting up our remix contest I did research from their point of view and learned about what THEY were asking for (not what I thought they wanted). Plus, I looked at many of the active and previously completed remix contests to identify the best elements for creating an effective and enticing presentation.

1. Where to Host Your Remix Contest:

There are several audio hosting sites out there but I chose SoundCloud for my contest as it provided everything I needed including free to low cost account options, built-in mechanisms for operating a remix contest along with an active community of remix producers.

They even provide the following blog of Step-by-Step instructions for creating a Remix Contest on SoundCloud. http://blog.soundcloud.com/2010/02/23/remix-competition/

As part of the steps outlined above, you will be creating a landing page that provides greater flexibility with your presentation and will be the link used for promoting your contest online. SoundCloud not only provides the essential management tools needed for a successful contest, but they also allow you to embed these functions into your website creating a seamless connection between their site and yours.

ex. http://www.chordsoftruth.com/remixed

2. Song Packs:

One of the items that many producers are asking for is a quick way to download all of the "stems" (or individual tracks) along with the original song all in one zip file called a "song pack". You can host these zip files on any of the popular file sharing sites (ex. Dropbox, Onlinefilefolder) then create a short url (bit.ly, goo.gl) to track the downloads.

One additional item I included in my song packs was a chords/lyrics sheet as a guide for the producers. This actually came in handy as many of the remix producers that participate in the contests do not primarily speak English so this helped them with syncing the vocals.

3. Rules (Terms & Conditions):

This is a very important aspect of the contest, and there is not a standard way to set these up. Once again it is best to research other contests and see what they have done and then decide which elements are appropriate and important for you. This would include items like a specific submission deadline, prizes, how the winners will be selected and under what creative commons license you are making the stems available.

For example, if you want to allow your stems to be shared and remixed, but want to retain control of the commercial aspects of them you want to use this license.

http://creativecommons.org/licenses/by-nc/3.0/

4. Prizes:

There are many different types of prizes that can be offered and you have to determine what is best for your situation. I decided to offer cash prizes, but found examples of everything from autographed merchandise to remixes being included on a major studio release to even studio time. It depends on what your resources are and what you're trying to accomplish with your contest. I also offered a free CD to the first 6 entries to encourage contest submissions well before the deadline.

5. Promote your Contest:

There has been an increase in remix contest sites appearing online recently, but many of them require significant minimum prize levels or even being involved with a label for inclusion. I did find a couple high traffic sites that are available for independent artists where a lot of producers go to find quality contest. Just be sure to follow the tips provided here to create a professional and appealing contest before submitting to increase your chances of getting a listing. Most of these sites are run by music fans that have made everything available simply because they enjoy it and if you don't provide something their users will like then they might not post your contest. And you would miss a good opportunity for exposure.

Here are a couple really good sites to submit to.
http://www.remixcomps.com
http://www.laptoprockers.eu

Another effective strategy for promoting your contest is to browse SoundCloud, listening to remixes and locating producers that have created remixes of a quality and style that you like. Then either comment on their remix or contact them through a private message letting them know that you like their work and that you have a remix contest. Just be considerate and do not spam.

6. Selecting the Winners:

There are many factors to consider when deciding who should be the winner of your contest, but in the end you should choose the remixes YOU like the most. There are mixed opinions on the web about considering things like comments, favorites, etc...but all of these can be manipulated and should only be considered a useful guide. Ultimately, your fans will be listening to these remixes and most people will only listen to who you chose as the winners. So you want them to be what reflects your tastes and is a good representation of your contest.

7. Announcing the Winners:

Once you have determined who the winners will be you will want to update your landing page with a personal message about the contest explaining how you came to the decisions. One thing you'll find is that this is much harder than you might think. All of the contestants have put time and effort into your contest and all but a few of them will be left empty handed. Of course they are aware of this going in but it doesn't make it any easier to leave anyone out.

Many of them are new fans of your music which is why they decided to work with your songs in the first place. So be sure to personally contact each of them thanking them for participating and complimenting aspects of their remix so they know that you listened to and truly considered their hard work for the prize. I even ended up selecting additional "Finalists" to recognize and awarded small prizes beyond what I had originally advertised because it was too difficult to cut it off at just 2 winners.

You also want to post the announcement with a link to the landing page on all of your social networks along with a short blurb on press release sites. The promotional work that you did for the contest will continue to generate traffic to the landing page even after the contest is over. So how you handle this aspect of the contest will resonate beyond just the contest and can help you generate new fans even after the contest is over.

8. Release a Compilation Album:

[135]

Depending on the quality and quantity of selections you receive, it may be possible to create a new album of remixes (even a few would justify an EP). I offered the participating producers a 25% cut of all profits generated from their remix (sales, royalties, etc...), but offered the album as a free download through the website and the individual remixes are available to download through SoundCloud. I also registered the album with CDBaby to make the tracks available for sale on iTunes, Amazon, and other online retailers along with being added to the Rumblefish database for potential sync licensing in movies, commercials, etc...

You will not only have the potential of reaching an entirely new audience of electronic music fans but it also creates exposure for your band and the original songs. Many of the same promotional strategies outlined in this ebook can be used to complement what you're already doing with your original material to increase the reach and effectiveness of your campaigns.

Music Video Contests

The other type of contest that will gain exposure for your music and get the fans involved is a music video contest. Many of the same steps are involved with a video contest.

1. Where to Host Your Music Video Contest:

The largest and most popular video hosting site is of course, YouTube. They offer the ability for fans to upload videos to their own accounts and then you can add them to a contest playlist on your Channel. This not only allows your fans to easily find the contest entries through your Channel, but also exposes your music to the existing fan base of the video creator as an audience as well.

Another benefit of using YouTube is that they have just recently improved their ability to license and monetize music that has been registered with Rumblefish through a site called Friendlymusic. http://friendlymusic.com

[136]

If you register your music with CDBaby, they have secured a partnership with Rumblefish to include your songs in this mechanism. So when a fan uploads a music video using one of your songs it is tagged as being owned by Rumblefish (which is you) and ads will be displayed with your video generating profits that will eventually filter back to you as income.

If you are looking for a different site to host your contest another good option is Vimeo (this is what we used). They are a growing community of creative video artists that do not allow copyrighted, commercial or marketing videos of any kind. They offer the ability to create a group and then submissions can be uploaded to their free Vimeo account and added to your Contest group.

2. What Content to Provide:

There are many different styles of music videos that could be created and it is important to decide what you are looking for in order to help guide the submissions. For example, do you want to provide footage of your band or would you rather have them create a personal vision of your music by scripting and shooting new footage, using stock footage/photos, or even animations/visualizations.

If you decide to provide band footage you will more than likely receive only submissions using it because regardless of the other options there will be an assumption that this is what you want. On the flipside, if you do not include this footage they will have no choice but to create something without your image involved. It just depends on what you're looking for.

I decided to leave us out of the videos and provided links to free stock footage sites, made suggestions for styles and gave examples of videos we liked from other bands that could be created using the type of content available for our contest.

3. Create a Landing Page:

Once again you will want to create a landing page for your contest that will allow greater flexibility in your presentation that will be the link used for promoting your contest.

This page should include a full explanation about what you are looking for in a music video, how the contest works, what the rules and prizes are along with how you will decide on the winners. Ex. http://www.chordsoftruth.com/videocontest

Something else that I did was record a personal video message explaining the details of the contest, posted it on YouTube and embedded it at the top of the landing page. This helps to clarify what you are looking for and creates a personal connection between the band and the fans. Plus it increases the potential for your contest to be discovered through the video hosting sites.

4. Promote your Contest:

There are also many sites for promoting video contests available. Many of these sites have minimum prize levels and high standards for who they include as well. The best strategy here is to search the web as someone looking for contests and then find the sites and submission guidelines where you would be a good fit.

This is a great site that offered a free listing along with a premium option for $75, which provided the ability to add images to your post along with additional exposure on the site. http://www.onlinevideocontests.com

You will also want to browse sites for videos that you like and contact the creators about your contest. Just be sure not to imply anything that would create a false expectation in their mind about winning. Remember that most contestants will not receive a prize.

5. Selecting and Announcing the Winners:

There are so many different aspects to consider when selecting the winners but in the end you should choose the one that best represents you and your music. When fans come to check out your contest results these will be the videos they watch most of the time. You will want to update your landing page with a personal message explaining how you decided on the winners along with embedding the videos in your landing page for easy viewing. Post the results with a link to your landing page on all of your social media accounts and create a press release.

It is also important to send a personal message to each contestant about their video thanking them for participating. Once again, they probably created the video because your song inspired them and they will want to know you enjoyed their video and appreciate their hard work.

Contests are a great way to get your fans involved and to have unique content created with your music on a limited budget. But it is crucial for you to be professional and to make the experience fun for everyone that decides to become involved.

INDEPENDENT ARTISTS WORKING BRILLIANTLY TOWARDS SUCCESS

Guest Article by Samuel Marcus & Jennifer Thorington
Music PR, Licensing, Development & Production
www.workingbrilliantly.com

Indie artists in today's world have a huge advantage. Music promotion and sales are now in their court and the control of their careers are in their hands. This is a blessing to most, since the creative control and success of their music is reliant on their personal overall focus, determination and belief in themselves versus a huge record label controlling all aspects of their lives. But, on the other hand, it poses a problem for those artists who have a harder time organizing themselves or running the business side of their career. Thankfully, there are many options available to help with this, such as managers, PR companies and sites like Reverbnation and Constant Contact that help organize their fans, assist with press outreach, promote new releases, videos, etc. and keep all their information in one easy place. Websites are even easier to build and financial support can be raised through sites like Wix and Kickstarter.

Financial success is a huge factor in an artist's ability to pursue their art full time. It is more than possible in this day and age for an independent artist to not only recoup their investment, but also support a lifestyle that is in alignment with what they dream for themselves. It takes time, focus, perseverance, work, creativity and unwavering confidence in their ability to succeed.

We have noticed over the years that a stumbling block for musicians is giving up or letting go of a project too soon. Now this is not a bid to get independent musicians deeper into financial debt with their project, but a simple philosophy on perseverance:

[140]

A release has a long shelf life. A client will too often give up on their project because a) they have had little return from the press world b) they have had a discouraging response from press or c) they are overly excited about their new project and are therefore dismissive of their previous one.

The truth is that press is a cumulative process in which you or your manager or publicist works their ass off to get peoples' attention. Unless you are working with payola outlets or have some insanely juicy publicity angle, good music takes a while to get heard, processed and put into print. More often than not, you have to water the proverbial flower and over time it will, indeed, bloom into something impressionable. That is unless you stomp on the sprout before it fully forms.

Another good analogy is that of drops of water in a pond. The ramifications of releasing an album occur over time, echoing out into the world through exposure and word of mouth. The more drops of water, the bigger the impact, the more chances to reach the shore.

Artists should be supporting their release in as many creative ways as possible. One idea could be to create a music video to support every song on the album and each video should be publicized in a compelling way, bringing people back to the album via interest in the video. Another could be simply visiting different hangouts on the Internet; starting clever conversations with potential fans and channeling them back to an amazingly well put together web site.

The biggest success we have seen is with bands that put out their material and don't look back. That is to say, they never question if they did the right thing, letting the chips fall where they may. That doesn't mean they neglect their release, it means they move forward into more endeavors that support it like touring, viral media, positive thinking and continual fan and press outreach.

[141]

RESOURCES

Y ou may want to search the relevant online directories or pick up the latest Indie Band Bible, but here are some sites you will definitely want to check out for further research. Instead of simply sharing a typical "top 50 music blogs" list, I wanted to share something a bit more personal.

Many of the resources and publications listed below are ones that actually support independent artists. The problem with most musician resources lists is that the sites themselves are generally inaccessible to outsiders, preferring to make their presence online an exercise in snobbery. This is not the case with most of the list below. While this small list is no replacement for the directories you should be seeking out, I hope that these add some serious arsenal to your promotional tool belt.

Hypebot – www.hypebot.com

Hypebot is one of the most informative music business websites currently on the net. Keep a close eye on this site for industry news, music marketing advice, and opinions from various knowledgeable sources.

Music Think Tank – www.musicthinktank.com

Owned and edited by the same person as Hypebot, Music Think Tank offers endless insight into music promotion, with fresh content from both regular and guest posters.

Berklee School of Music - www.berkleemusic.com

Berklee is a very respected music school with courses covering everything from song writing to the music business.

DIY Musician from CDBaby

http://diymusician.cdbaby.com/

Relevant and simple advice from CDBaby's blog.

Make It In Music – www.makeitinmusic.com

Another informative industry advice website.

The Indie Bible – www.indiebible.com

The Indie Bible provides an excellent resource for independent artists looking for reviews, airplay, distribution, press or advice. To go beyond the music blogs checklist that Hype Machine will offer, pick up a copy.

The Indie Venue Bible – www.indiebible.com

The Indie Venue Bible is a comprehensive venue database created to assist independent musicians with the tough job of booking tours. If you are planning a tour on your own, this is another MUST HAVE. Released by the Indie Bible team, this book is specifically for touring artists and contains more venues than you could possibly ever play. Even better, the venues are expecting you to get in touch.

Artists in Music Awards – www.aimusicawards.com

Founded Mikey Jayy has a deep passion for independent music of all genres, and he dedicates his days and nights to promoting it through his popular radio show and his Los Angeles-based Artists in Music Awards, which is open to artists of all genres worldwide.

Music XRay – www.musicxray.com

Music XRay is a A & R and opportunities website for independent musicians. Artists can submit their music for major record label consideration, licensing (film, video game, tv) opportunities, consultations, reviews, airplay, promotional campaigns and press coverage just to name a few.

WHOA Magazine – www.whoamagazine.co

Ever since I first started working with WHOA Magazine, the drive and enthusiasm of CEO Anthony "Train" Caruso has blown me away. They are one of the few publications at their level who are genuinely open to independent artists. In fact, they fill their pages with them as well as interview them every weekday on their WHOA 100 Radio show. With the new WHOA Label launched, there's no stopping this company.

Jamsphere Magazine – www.jamsphere.com

Jamsphere is a multi-faceted company who I have had nothing but wonderful experiences with. Dedicated to the success of independent artists to the point that their services are constantly expanding their reach, you can be guaranteed that all quality artists are given a fair chance here. They syndicate their reviews to ensure added exposure. Coupled with their radio show and corresponding website, their brand new magazine and low advertising rates, Jamsphere.com is a highly recommended hub for any serious independent artist.

I Am Entertainment Magazine - www.iaemagazine.com

They're ambitious and they run a very professional publication. They also provide independent artists with one of the best opportunities for both reviews and advertising, with among the lowest and most reasonable rates I've seen. Taking care of the other side of the business, they properly promote their magazine, recently going into print in a time when most are shying away.

Middle Tennessee Music – www.midtnmusic.com

Middle Tennessee Music is chalk full of valuable advice for musicians. They also provide high quality artist reviews and interviews as well.

Vandala Concepts Magazine – www.vandalaconcepts.com

This publication is open to independent artists, and cover as many as any other I've seen. On top of this, they provide just about every service imaginable to serious artists.

SKOPE Magazine – www.skopemag.com

SKOPE Magazine is another publication dedicated solely to independent music. They actually give independent artists a chance, so this is a great place to start for any artist looking for exposure or advertising.

Penseyeview – www.penseyeview.com

One of our favourite publications and an excellent supporter of independent music through their daily music features.

Target Audience Magazine
www.targetaudiencemagazine.com

Covering a mixture of major and independent artists, I've had nothing but positive experiences with Target Audience Magazine. I encourage you to read and support the publication.

This Is Vibes – www.thisisvibes.com

An independent music site spanning all genres with a special focus on hip hop and r&b.

Music Emissions – www.musicemissions.com

Music Emissions is a massive independent music community reviewing both indie and major artists. They offer paid reviews and the service is very professional.

Indie Band Guru – www.indiebandguru.com

Exactly as the title suggests, site creator Keith Pro is the real deal, always striving to help indie acts.

The Real Musician – www.therealmusician.com

Offering everything from music marketing advice to an in-depth guide to producing music with Reason, Andrew Muller's The Real Musician website has grown into a high traffic institution for a reason. It's helpful.

All Songs Considered

http://www.npr.org/programs/asc/submissions/

All Songs Considered is a high influential program put on by NPR, and they give all artists a chance. Be sure to follow the instructions to a tee, and make sure your product is ready.

Kings of A&R – www.kingsofar.com

Kings of A&R is very popular publication. Artists featured here often move on to big things.

Musicperk – www.musicperk.com

Many artists make the mistake of sticking to their home town when looking for press. Few think to look towards India, where one of the coolest and most helpful websites, Musicperk, can be found.

Totally Fuzzy – www.totallyfuzzy.blogspot.com

Totally Fuzzy is the name. Music discovery is the game. Have an album stream ready? How about a new music video? This is the website for you.

Hellhound Music – www.hellhoundmusic.com

Hellhound Music is a top notch rock (and surrounding genres) website without any snobbery whatsoever. They're a friendly and enthusiastic group of folks who in my experience have an extremely positive attitude towards independent acts.

Ultima Music Blog – www.ultimamusicblog.net
Covering rock, electronic, industrial, metal, punk, progressive and surrounding genres, Ultima is a wonderful publication.

Feedback Fury – www.feedbackfury.com
Fast and furious, this rock, punk, alternative and metal website gained attention by conducting unique interviews with up-and-coming artists, as well as stars like Henry Rollins.

Speakercone – www.speakercone.net
Offering a wide range of services for independent artists, Speakercone is run by Michael Finney, a musician and entrepreneur who loves passionate artists.

Ampkicker – www.ampkicker.com
They've been supporting indie bands since their inception and show no signs of slowing down.

Music Review Unsigned – www.musicreviewunsigned.com
One of the best independent music publications online.

Blog Critics – www.blogcritics.com
They cater to all genres. Seek out a reviewer and contact him with a pitch.

Spoutfire – www.spoutfire.com
Send in your submissions for their 'Music Interlude' section.

Vents Magazine – www.ventsmagazine.com
Covering all genres and very much open to independent acts.

Bandbucket.com – www.bandbucket.com
Opportunities abound on this alternative music site.

The Noise Beneath the Apple
www.thenoisebeneaththeapple.com
Wonderful independent music website covering artists in New York and internationally, with an added focus on the art of busking.

Nanobot Rock – www.nanobotrock.com
High quality and very approachable music review site supporting quality independent artists.

Music Connection Magazine – www.musicconnection.com
Join their AMP network to get reviewed.

Technorati Music Blogs Database
http://technorati.com/blogs/directory/entertainment/music/
Technorati is the largest blog tracker in the world. Their music blog database has 8,000 music blogs. It's VERY possible that some of them would be interested in your band.

No Depression – www.nodepression.com
No Depression is a hub for the country and Americana music communities. This very popular publication has turned itself into a social network where independent musicians are encouraged to sign up and post their music and news releases. Don't hesitate to contact the industry professionals and reviewers who frequent the site.

Garageband – www.garageband.com
The world's largest independent music community. This site offers the potential to get reviewed by new fans and fellow musicians.

Drowned in Sound – www.drownedinsound.com
Appeal to the individual reviewers here. This site is lucrative and influential.

Blabbermouth – www.blabbermouth.net
Blabbermouth is a great place to break a press release for rock/metal bands. Get it posted here and it will mysteriously show up in a lot of other places.

Band Weblogs – www.bandweblogs.com
Band weblogs will post your press releases provided they are relevant and well-written. Make sure you return the generosity by making your releases newsworthy and informative.

Artist Direct – www.artistdirect.com
Get as involved as you can with this website. They offer a variety of features.

Antimusic – www.antimusic.com
We've found Antimusic to be an excellent rock music news website, and they accept news releases from bands. Even better, they offer features on independent artists.

Pure Grain Audio – www.puregrainaudio.com

This website supports indie artists, but unlike other "indie" sites, it has a wide audience, and garners press with many major artists as well. It's an excellent site to get involved with.

Chart Attack - www.chartattack.com

Contrary to the site's title, you don't need to be on the charts to be covered. Indie bands can be found all over this site.

MI2N - www.mi2n.com/

Ah yes! Post your press releases here and never look back!

Alternative Press – www.altpress.com

Another popular publication that covers indie bands in it's online format.

The Daily Swarm - www.thedailyswarm.com

Music news and headlines.

NPR – www.npr.org

Even though it's the top music site as ranked by Google, they do have a section called "All Songs Considered", which accepts independent music submissions.

Ultimate Guitar - www.ultimate-guitar.com/news

You do play guitar, right? Well, send them some news! Approach them with a relevant article idea.

Play Louder - www.playlouder.com

Music reviews and news website.

Taxi – www.taxi.com

"Get your music to the right people" is their slogan. Taxi works to get your music submitted for film, television or advertising placement. Give it a try and see if it works for you.

Large Hearted Boy - http://blog.largeheartedboy.com

If this boy digs you, you've got an audience.

Music for Robots - http://music.for-robots.com/

Music for Robots is an extremely popular indie music blog. This website provides a very helpful list of music blogs for you to promote to.

The rest of the thousands of places you should get in touch with can be found at the directories specified earlier. As a reminder, here are some of the best starting points:

The Hype Machine - http://hypem.com/list - Hype Machine is a truly awesome list of music blogs. Make sure they're relevant to your genre.

The Google directory

http://www.google.com/Top/Arts/Music/ - Check every nook and cranny.

The Indie Link Exchange - http://bigmeteor.com/ile/ - Either get involved or just contact the websites that are relevant to you.

THE TRUE ARTIST'S MAJOR MARKETING DILEMMA

(Courtesy of Target Audience Magazine)
www.targetaudiencemagazine.com)

By James Moore

Creative types have historically had a fair amount of trouble not only promoting their work, but also allowing it the chance to be promoted. As with many small businesses who soon close their doors, many writers, artists, musicians and film makers create a product, release it, and then "wait for the people to come". It's this notion of the process of "getting discovered" that needs to change in order for us to take up our own mantles and advance our creative endeavours.

One issue that I have seen again and again, even in myself, is a deep-seeded issue of perception. Throughout our lives we have all been overexposed to commercials of all motivations and persuasions. It's natural to be sick of it. We feel that the powers that be are lying to us or that everyone is trying to sell us something whether we need it or not. We feel trapped and without options, and this leads us to fantasize. We fantasize about heroes; people who stood up and gave a middle finger to the authorities in this world and refused to play by the rules. We liken ourselves to people who would never, ever lower themselves to the level of self-promotion.

Like many perceptions and beliefs that we hold true and dear, as George Gerschwin would say, "It ain't necessarily so."

I'd like to suggest that it may be possible to ruthlessly self-promote and also be a true artist. They just don't teach that in "Starving Artist 101". The Doors used to request their own songs on Los Angeles radio to get their music heard. If not for this effort, they may have remained relatively unknown and scattered off on their separate ways. Technically, what they did is cheating.

[150]

This is true according to many of the standards us creative types have adopted in the promotion of our works. And yet, they were true artists, and the fact that they promoted themselves in this way is far less than a footnote compared to what became their enduring legacy.

Even the great Salvador Dali ruthlessly self-promoted his own work as well as his political ideas by collaborating with like minds to form a movement, in the process embracing controversy and eccentricity as a marketing technique. Of course, he was promoting his real self. However, it's still promotion in the end.

This is where most creative people get stuck. Partially because of the glitzy imagery shown to us by the music industry over the past 50 years, we've become accustomed to the idea of great artists getting carted around in style while a team of industry experts worked to take care of the rest. I suppose that is why many of us finish our product or art piece, set up a website or a Wordpress blog, post our sales link on our Facebook profile, and then wait. We wait for our team to arrive. We wait for something to happen. And yet it doesn't. What we get to keep is our defensive nature. We get to keep the belief that we hold dearest – that no matter what happens, we know that we are true artists and we never sold out. But is that true? Is it possible that we simply never tried? Perhaps we have been following ideals that don't really exist.

It's critical for creative people to get past this hurdle, possibly more critical than anything else. Once the "true artist" illusion is removed, we are free to REALLY be true artists and give our work the respect it deserves by promoting it far and wide. That is not to say that spamming your friends repeatedly on social networks is going to get you anywhere, but if you can think like a business owner it will help the discovery of your work.

Using relatively new technologies such as the Wildfire application (www.wildfireapp.com), anyone can campaign creatively and virally, gaining potentially thousands of new followers in the process. Micro-job websites like Fiverr.com and Freelancer.com are becoming more and more popular for good reason. You can get almost anything done if you know where to look, and that includes getting press in the form of interviews and reviews, hiring someone to edit your novel, securing advertising for your product, or even having someone produce a video of themselves dancing to your song. Different strokes for different folks.

Dozens of blogs in your niche are looking for people to interview. This is often called 'unique content', and if you pitch yourself offering this, you are far more likely to score press. It essentially means less work for the blog owner because you are providing the content. Article writing and guest blogging are other tactics that many have adopted in their promotion strategies. And if no one wants to cover you, start your own blog! Write content and make it popular. This can give you leverage when promoting to other blogs within your niche because you now have something to offer in terms of cross-promotion. Uploading original videos to a YouTube channel and joining YouTube's partner program can give you both popularity and extra revenue.

These are but a few of the dozens of techniques available, and there are more options every day. You can never really even scratch the surface. Use your intuition when choosing, but it's better to try everything than to try nothing. For those who can't get over their aversion to promotion, I would suggest keeping your art strictly as a hobby, because when you make a habit of dipping your toe in the water only to stay on solid ground, it's merely a fearful exercise and nothing more.

INDUSTRY INTERVIEW
with Stuart Epps
(www.stuartepps.co.uk)

It was a true honour for me to have the chance to speak with the legendary record producer/engineer Stuart Epps, who has worked with artists such as Led Zeppelin, Elton John, George Harrison, Bill Wyman, Oasis, Twisted Sister, Robbie Williams, Jeff Beck, Paul Rodgers and many others. Starting his music career at the age of 15 in 1967, Stuart has over 40 years of first-hand experience in the ever-changing music industry.

Aspiring artists and producers alike should find this interview both sobering and inspiring. We talked about some of the main issues confronting the industry today and his answers were fascinating. The main message I personally took from it is that we all have sometimes rigid perceptions of what the "music industry" should be and what it owes us for our efforts, but, as George Gershwin would say, "It ain't necessarily so." Success in any facet of the business is difficult, but it is definitely possible. In some ways, not much has changed, and that should be a relief to many. Without further delay, Stuart Epps!

Mr. Epps, it's an honor to speak with you and thank you for your contributions to music. Please share with our readers what you've been up to lately. I understand that you accept independent artist submissions for production, mixing and mastering, which is a stellar opportunity.

Hi James. It's incredible, really. I've been in this business for 40 years now and I thought I'd seen everything, done everything and been everywhere, but it's the amazing thing about this business I'm in that I'm often finding myself in situations I haven't been in before; whether it's a different band, different music or different sounds, and obviously the music business is changing and has changed dramatically.

At the moment, via a great music website called Music XRay I have been mixing bands and artist's home recordings, which is something I never imagined I'd be doing. To be honest I got a bit fed up with lack of budgets and trying to get artists to record in commercial studios. Anyway, with the invention of the internet I'm in touch with bands and the internet has brought us together – musicians and artists and producers from all over the world.

So it's pooling resources, and what I'm finding myself doing now is taking the waves from artist's home recordings and mixing them, as well as sometimes adding my own production ideas such as adding other instruments and enhancing what they've already achieved, which is working out great. I'm enjoying doing it. Sometimes artists aren't the easiest to deal with face to face. This way I'm not always having to. Sometimes I don't even speak to anyone. We're just communicating via their music, which isn't a bad thing really. That's working out well and I've been very busy with that. I'm still working with artists in my own studio and in commercial studios but as I said, unfortunately budgets are on the decrease so remixing is a good way to "carry on the good work".

What is the best way for someone interested in music production to learn how to do what you do?

Interesting question because music is so huge now, really – bigger than ever before and everyone is making music it would seem. It's promoted on the TV with all your X Factor style shows where everyone is singing away and playing furiously, and live music is bigger than ever before. So everyone wants to learn how to be a music producer it would seem, and I've been lecturing to music schools via Skype in Canada and across the world about this. There are many thousands of colleges that are teaching engineering and music production and of course I'm all for it.

In my day, the only way to learn was really hands on starting at the bottom in a recording studio or a publisher. In my case it was a demo studio and you'd learn engineering and somehow work your way up. Obviously there is a lot more available now as you can actually go to schools to learn that. Hands on is the best way as well. With home recording facilities you can experiment at home, with your friends and with bands. I'm always talking about what separates an engineer from someone who wants to do music production. It's a fascinating subject which is too lengthy to go into here, but they are very different things to learn how to do. For music production, the best thing to do would be to go to a college and jump into it as soon as possible with friends, with bands, with home recording, and learn as much as you can.

Please share your thoughts on the controversial issue of free file sharing and its effects on independent artists.

With the invention of the internet it's incredible that you can record a demo or a track in the morning and by the evening have it finished, then promote it through all the various music sites. Of course I think that it would be nice to make money out of it, but at that early stage I think just getting people to listen is a good thing, really. There's so much music out there that you can't really charge for these things until you become a little bit more well-known and maybe your music has evolved and gotten that much better. Then, maybe you can charge for it, but that's just the same as it was in the 60's and 70's.

A new band starting out was not likely to get paid in a pub or a club. If they made a demo, they probably would have to pay for it. Good luck trying to sell it, too. It's not really any different in that respect. It's just that everyone assumes these days that if you make something one day you should be able to sell it the next day somewhere or other. The main thing is – none of us really thought about the money when we were making music in the 60's or 70's. If you start out at age 15 or 16 or even earlier, you're not thinking in monetary terms. You're just thinking "I want to play music", and if money comes along that's a complete bonus, but this was when the music industry was in its infancy. It wasn't

[155]

such a huge industry as it is now. I understand that everyone wants to make money from it but I think the fact is that there are so many more people listening to music than ever before. It's become a cheaper item. The whole thing has been cheapened to a certain extent, but because it's in such vast quantities it sort of makes up for it in that respect.

Is the music industry evolving or collapsing? Does it matter?

It's definitely evolving. It's always been evolving. Revolving and evolving…it's probably more revolving now as music just seems to go around in circles with the technology and the different styles of bands. It does seem that there's very little that comes along now that seems to be completely new. It always seems to be somewhat of a rehash of some of the old music. It's just reinvented. People say that the music industry is finished or has collapsed, and certainly the old music industry has collapsed pretty much. The giant record companies are obviously feeling the pressure from the internet, and that's a good thing, really. The only way that you could get a record deal or get your music heard in my day was through a record company or a publisher and very much through the establishment that was set up, which was hard to break into.

Now artists can record a record in their bedroom in the morning and have it beamed out to whoever is there to listen by the evening. That's something that didn't exist when I started, so it's definitely evolving. It's difficult to make money from making records, I suppose. That's what we're talking about. It's not difficult to make music and it's not difficult to get it heard, really. You can have your own radio station if there are people there to listen. It's possible.

Making money out of the music business and making it a career is not so easy, but then again it never was. Just like any other industry it's very difficult. I would say that it's an extremely exciting time. The live music industry is bigger than ever. There are more bands. There are more artists. There's more people playing live than ever before, and that's an incredible thing. Who would have thought that would have ever been the case in the

60's, or certainly the 80's when it was mainly electronic music. So that's a great thing and I think that the music industry at the moment is more exciting than ever.

Many artists don't seem to know how to promote themselves properly. What are some of the most common mistakes you see artists make all the time?

It's very difficult. I tend to go for the old, traditional ways which are music publishers and record companies, but then obviously there's MySpace and Facebook. There are literally hundreds of thousands of ways for the individual to promote themselves across the internet with all the various music sites. I think it takes the same tenacity that was needed years ago. The only thing is, life is a bit easier now generally.

People aren't as ruthless now as they used to be in getting their music heard. It was a question of getting out of the house. "How do I get out of the house? How do I leave home? I'm going to go join a band and we'll tour all over the place as long as we don't have to be at home, and as long as we're playing our music". I think that some of that has gone out of individual artists ideas, really. I mean, everyone thinks that you can just make a record in the morning and tomorrow it will be number 1; everyone will be buying it and everyone will be watching you on YouTube and you'll be on X Factor, and everyone tends to want immediate success without putting in as much of the hard work and technical ability or musicality that is required to make great music. It's only when you make great music that you will get a great reaction, and you'll find that you probably don't have to promote yourself.

A lot of the artists that I work with – it took them years, really, to achieve any sort of status. You've got to be dedicated and single-minded. Never give up and never let anything stand in your way. These are the things that are required to help promote your music.

It seems that you have found innovative and collaborative ways to continuously be successful with what you do. Do you have any advice for young producers as well as artists who may be stuck in old models of thinking? (For example, many artists obsess over the decrease of album sales but fail to educate themselves on the benefits of licensing or advertising.)

If we're talking about well-known bands, it is a fact that record sales have decreased. There is a lot of pirating and downloading that still goes on, so obviously even the successful bands aren't selling in the quantities they used to. At the same time, ticket sales are absolutely huge for big bands and that's become the new way for artists to make money. In the early days, the gig was really a promotional tool for the CD and now that's completely reversed. The CD is the promotional tool for the live gig, where then the famous band can go ahead and charge $200 a ticket whereas the CD is only likely to be $20, so it's changed a lot in that respect. I mean, it's always been about promotion. That's where the record companies were vital, really…that whole system of signing a new artist, nurturing them, paying for it as it went along, recording demos, promoting…

I was in there working with Elton John right from the beginning working for Dick James, and a whole team of us…40, 50 people working every day, really, to try and make Elton John a famous artist and to increase record sales, and his whole career, so it's not an easy situation for someone to do on their own. It's almost impossible I would say, but if you're determined enough and you use the tools that are available (which weren't available then), you just have to keep at it and it's possible to get your name out there. You've got to be very dedicated, and beyond all those things, it's about having a great product. You have to have a product that stands out not necessarily quality wise or production wise but depth-wise, the writing and the musicianship. Any great artist who has the right tools will come through in the end. It's just a matter of time.

Is music more difficult to promote these days? Do you feel the market is oversaturated?

It's a very good question. When I started off, music was not something that everyone was into and I suppose you felt that you were part of a select few that made music or recorded music.

Maybe there was that magic about it, the idea that "it's only us that know about it", and now everyone seems to be talking about it. If we had a pair of headphones to listen to music with, that was unusual. Now you get on the train and everyone has got a pair of headphones on, but I just think it's great actually. It's just great to see everyone doing what we hoped everyone would do, and that's listening to music and making music.

I don't know about the term 'oversaturated'. There's a lot of still not very good music and there's very few things that ARE great. Maybe that's a good thing as well. To make great music and be a great artist isn't easy. It is difficult. It IS possible but it still takes the same amount of talent that it always took, and you still can't "make a silk purse out of a pig's ear", so to speak. No matter what technology comes along, it's still not possible to be great unless you are truly great. It's just like any other art, really, whether it's painting or sculpting. It doesn't matter how many people have a go at it. There's still only going to be certain people who will succeed at it and are great at it. It doesn't matter how many people make music or get involved in music. It seems that quality wins out in the end…hopefully.

You've worked with some of the greats such as Led Zeppelin and Elton John. In your opinion, is musical greatness something that has to come about naturally, or is tenacity the necessary ingredient?

It's a great question, and I'm lucky to say that having seen it happen, I think I have an answer. Of course, musical talent is important first and foremost. Being a great singer, songwriter, and musician – if you have all those 3 that's very, very rare but that's definitely going to get you somewhere. That's for sure. If you're a great singer, songwriter and a great performer that's when you get the greats. You mentioned Elton John and Led Zeppelin, some of the greats who I've been fortunate enough to work with – they had those 3 talents. But also, extremely important and just as important, if not more important, is determination, having an inner strength and a wanting to succeed in the business of music. To have it happen. To make it big. To question everything, really.

If you do that all the way along the line then chances are you will come out with something special. If you're writing a song and you think "No, it's got to be better. It's got to be better. It can still be better." then you'll write a better song. If you're trying to become a better singer, you hear yourself recorded and you think "No, I can sing better than that. I want to sing better than that. I'm going to sing better than that." Same with guitar playing, piano playing, drums – everything. It's critical as a musician to get better and better.

Some things I find difficult with young musicians if they want to be great at everything. They want to be a great drummer and a great singer and a great producer and a great engineer. They seem to want to be good at every part of every facet of the music business, which isn't the case with some of those people I've mentioned. In the early days, musicians let managers and producers get on with what they did while they got on with what they did the best they knew how, and I think that's something to learn from, really. Get as good as you can at your instrument, your song writing, and question it all the time.

I mean, Jimmy Page – you mentioned Led Zeppelin, I know that he never achieved what he wanted to achieve in the studio. None of these artists fully achieved it. It was always the striving to get that perfection, and that's what makes for great music and great artists.

What do you look for in artists you choose to work with?

Sometimes it tends to be the other way around these days. Artists choose me, but I'm always looking for a great song. I'm always looking for a great musician. Of course I'm always thinking "Is this going to be the new Beatles?" The new Led Zeppelin - I would love to find. Where is the next Led Zeppelin? Where is a band that even sounds anything like Led Zeppelin or Bad Company or any of the great bands from the 60's or 70's? They just don't seem to exist. They don't seem to stay together long enough to fully exist anyway. I mean, bands are really difficult to be in and difficult to get along with if you're a member of a band so it takes a lot of work to make a band successful and I don't think people work at it enough.

Basically, I try to clear my head and I listen to the artist hoping it's going to be something I like and something I think I can add to; that's more the case. If a band or an artist does come up and their sound is great and everything seems fine, the arrangement is all there and there's not much for me to do then that's great, but obviously not great from my point of view.

So, I'm looking for all sorts of things when I listen to a new artist for the first time. Working with Music XRay, I'm working with bands from Australia, the U.S, Canada, South America, South Africa, all over the world really. There does seem to be a common element in music when it comes to rock music. We all seem to like the same things. That is a great feeling, really. Coming up to nearly 60 years old, it's not something I imagined would happen. None of us imagined when we were in our 20's that the new generation would in any way like the music that we liked. To be in this era where everybody writes down their favourite band and its Led Zeppelin and we're still talking about bands and rock music. It's a great thing, really, and I'm just happy to be in it.

Very few people seem to understand the music industry. Can you leave us with some advice for anyone looking to follow their dreams and make music their career?

It's a very wide subject, isn't it (the music industry)? I do Skype conferences with music students of all ages, but people seem to wait until older and older ages before they even start to learn. I say it's best to start as early as possible. I started in the music business when I was 15 and I don't think you can start early enough. I also think that it's important to know as early as possible which area of the music business that you want to join, and to get into that and to learn all about that and not try to learn every facet of it or learn what everyone else's jobs are. Admittedly, if you want to become a record producer it's good to learn engineering. It's good to be grounded in that, but if you know that you're a great guitarist and you love playing guitar I think it's best to stick to learning that instrument and doing it the best you can.

Jimmy Page, I mean, he was one of the top session musicians at age 15 or 16. He had been playing since he was a little boy. He wanted to play that guitar and know absolutely everything about it. Of course, he became a really good record producer and got into that side of things, but still, he was learning and wanted to put together a great band. A lot of the musicians that I've worked with...Paul Rogers just wanted to be a great singer. I find that some of the new bands that are great tend to specialize. Coming back to the question, that's what I think. It's good to find out early on what you're going to be best at and then honing in on that. Obviously if it's a musician then that's getting together with other musicians, getting your craft together, writing great songs.

People tend to work on their own too much these days. Sometimes you can't do everything yourself. Sometimes you're going to need a lyricist even if you're a great songwriter like Elton John. His lyrics weren't good at all when I first worked with him before he met Bernie Taupin. Sometimes you have to work with others in order to get it even better. It's a great music industry, still. Get into it as soon as possible, I say.

To get in touch with Stuart Epps regarding your music, please visit:

Stuart's official website - www.stuartepps.co.uk

Stuart's XRay profile: www.musicxray.com/profiles/943

INTERVIEW WITH ANDY GESNER OF
HIP VIDEO PROMO

Andy Gesner is the CEO of the popular and successful music video distribution and promotion company HIP Video Promo (www.hipvideopromo.com). They've worked with clients both major and indie, and maintain a strong DIY ethos in their business practises. The purpose of this interview is to cover critical information in the area of music videos and their promotion.

"Hi Andy. So what is music video distribution anyway?"

"As a music video promoter for 12 years, I've learned just how valuable we are to our clients and record labels we work for. We're quite often referred to as their "scrubbing bubbles"... we do all the mind numbing work so our clients don't have to! A successful music video campaign involves lots of upfront costs and technical attention to detail. Whether a video is delivered digitally or on a tape format like a digi-beta or DV cam, you need to be 100% sure that there are no video hits, audio glitches or aspect ratio problems when the video arrives to the programmer.

What's more, you want to make sure the video is accompanied by a professionally written, compelling one sheet that gives the programmers all of the reasons why this is a video he or she needs to pay attention to, void of empty hype or false accolades. Once the video has arrived to the programmers, the most important step of any successful music video campaign is tenacious follow-up. We do lean on our programmers to give the programming love to our clients, but we are never arm twisty in our approach. We understand that a programmer has to genuinely be excited about the artist and video on their end, but because we are very selective about the videos we promote, we're usually confident that what we're presenting them is fully worthy of theirs and their viewer's attention.

[163]

"You've built a strong reputation at HIP Video Promo for working with major artists (Johnny Cash, Bon Iver, Death Cab for Cutie), up-and-coming indie artists, as well as major media outlets. Please tell us a bit about your business philosophy."

"Our business philosophy is very simple. Our goal is to supply our programmers with the videos their viewers really want to see. This leads to us declining many videos that are presented to us, because in the music video world, you never get a second chance to make a first impression. We are very blessed to get to work with some of the best independent record labels on the planet. But my greatest joy is to unearth the brand-new noteworthy independent artists that have up until this point, flew decidedly under the radar."

"What are some of the qualities you look for in a band and also a music video?"

"Now more than ever, the video does the talking! A band or artist can be just starting out, or barely established, but if the video is memorable and the song is good, lots of new potential fans will find out about you. It's also very helpful when the band or artist that we are working with have other parts of their marketing campaign working in tandem with us. Quite often when we were promoting a music video, the band or artist is running an online marketing campaign along with a press campaign and a radio campaign. Certainly the more pistons you can have pumping at once, the better chance you have of making an impact."

"Why is it necessary in 2012 and beyond for an independent artist to have a professionally done music video?"

"When I started HIP Video Promo in October of 2000, a professional music video was an expensive undertaking. But with the cost of digital filmmaking being lower than it's ever been, coupled with the fact that digital can often times look even better than film, has made a music video affordable for even the most independent of bands and artists. The video doesn't need to be expensive to be memorable. "

"Our most successful video campaigns have usually been videos that have a novel or compelling idea. Sometimes videos that are expensive end up falling short. And now more than ever, animated videos have really made a comeback. Quite often when a band or artist is on the road and doesn't have time to make a video, they can consider having an animated video, which doesn't require them being involved in any way, shape or form. There is no escaping the fact that now we live in a very video centric world. Fans of music also have a very short attention span. A well shot, compelling music video is the best way to connect with them...visually, musically and artistically."

"Most bands and artists shoot a video, put it straight on their social networks and Youtube, and then begin the cycle of looking for views wherever they can find them. What's missing from the master plan here? Why do you think proper video promotion falls by the wayside in most cases?"

"Upcoming bands and artists immediately think that professional music video promotion does not fit into their budget, or because of budgetary constraints, don't think they can afford our services. If a tree falls in the woods and no one is there to hear it, does it make a sound? If you really have an outstanding music video, you're selling yourself short if you don't get it out there to all the potential outlets that could give your video serious consideration for programming. It does require a lot of up front attention to detail, and this is the kind of thing best left to the professionals. So many of my programmers complain they get dozens of videos each month, but either the tape doesn't work right, it's not dubbed in stereo, it's not closed captioned, or the aspect ratio isn't right. That means that these folks have sent all these videos out, and no one's going to be able to play them. Because we've promoted so many videos, we've got a system down with excruciatingly stringent quality control. We are always confident that the videos that hit our programmer's desks are 100% ready for immediate programming. Sure, the cost of admission into our tent is not a small amount, but if you put a lot

[165]

of time and effort and money into producing a music video, it makes no sense to just have it sit on your YouTube page."

"What's involved when HIP Video Promo distributes and promotes a music video? Let's say you've approved a new artist, their video looks great and they want to reach all the outlets possible."

"The first thing we need to happen is to have the video delivered directly to us digitally. Once it is received, we need to check it out and make sure there are no technical issues before we move forward. The client must also provide us with lyrics for closed captioning, submission form info and graphic assets. At that point we prepare a music video promotion one sheet that is then approved by the client. Once all the duplication has taken place the campaign begins. We mail out all of our videos priority and first-class mail, and then there is about a three day waiting period until the programmers have received the video. Our campaigns last eight to ten weeks, and we report back to the client every two weeks with all the airplay that has been secured during that time frame. All throughout the campaign we are blogging, tweeting, and face booking about the artists, as well as placing phone calls to our most important programmers to encourage them to support the campaign."

"What advice would you give independent artists who want to plan, shoot, release, and promote a music video properly?"

"Just remember; you don't get a second chance to make a first impression!"

"What are the most common mistakes you see independent artists make today, both in the music video spectrum and in general?"

"In the music video spectrum, there are lots of common mistakes that independent artists are committing on a daily basis! Now that music videos are the best, most integral way of getting some traction on the independent musical landscape, bands and artists don't realize that the first video you unleash upon the unsuspecting public needs to be memorable, compelling, and leave an impression in the viewer's eyes that the band or artist are on the fast track to the next level. Quite often, if the first video leaves people unimpressed, they won't pay attention to a second or third video, even though they might be outstanding. Another common mistake is including "red flags" in their videos such as guns, drugs, salacious behavior, and naughty words.

"All of these red flags are going to limit airplay significantly, so it's best to stay away from them. Another common mistake is that they think they can't afford a service like ours, even though they spent a lot of money on the video. It seems that bands and artists shoot their entire load on shooting the video, and then have no extra money left to professionally promote it. If a band is really going to go all-out to produce an excellent music video, it makes no sense for them to just park it on their YouTube page or their Facebook page and that's it. You want to get it out there to all the potential programming outlets that might give it serious consideration for exposure. That's where a company like mine comes in to save the day!"

To find HIP Video Promo online as well as possibilities for your music video, visit www.hipvideopromo.com.

INTERVIEW WITH KATIE O'HALLORAN

Katie O'Halloran runs an A&R music blog at www.ithinkiloveit.com, and also works for EMI Publishing. I interviewed her in order to provide artists with helpful tips in those areas, where Katie has proven to be a wealth of knowledge…

"Welcome to Independent Music Promotions, Katie! Your music blog I Think I Love It (ithinkiloveit.com) is an A&R tip blog. What does this mean and what qualities do you look for when choosing artists to feature?"

"Thank you for having me, James. As an A&R tip blog, our aim is to turn industry gatekeepers onto new talent. As you might expect, our target audience includes labels and publishers, but we also strive to reach all industry players that have a reason to seek out emerging talent: Managers, agents, lawyers, PR people, music supervisors, media outlets, etc.

"We focus on unsigned artists as well as signed artists who are still relatively unknown (while the later might not be available for signing consideration, they could still be of interest to our readers for other purposes). In addition to artists, we cover emerging songwriters, producers, and DJs. With respect to style, the fact that we don't target one specific type of industry person or company leads to a diverse mix. For example, some of the talent we cover is super mainstream and in line with what majors are seeking. Others are more niche and in line with what music supervisors are seeking.

"When selecting artists to feature, our primary concern is the quality of the music. Quality is subjective, but in this context, I'm going to describe it as having commercial appeal. "Commercial appeal" doesn't mean it has to be cookie-cutter pop — if an artist writes songs that would never work at Top 40 radio, but would be perfect for advertisements, I would still categorize them as being commercial. In essence, we need to feel that their music could

[168]

realistically be put into some sort of significant income-generating situation. If they also have a defined image and noteworthy buzz, that's icing on the cake."

"You also work for EMI Music Publishing. Can you share with us a bit about your role and also some of the lessons you've learned taking on that role?"

"I work at the Canadian office, and much of my role is related to creative matters: Scouting for new talent, setting our office up with new A&R tools (like MusicClout and MusicXray), and working with the talent we already have (arranging collaborations, pitching their songs for various opportunities, etc.). However, I also get to jump around in other areas. For example, I manage our office's social media presence, prepare internal announcements, create bios and other press materials for our roster, work to secure media coverage for our roster, and help out with anything else the team needs of me.

"No matter how much you study the industry before diving in, there are some things you just won't find in a book. Since I started working at EMI Music Publishing (EMIMP), I've been able to learn from the company-specific strategies that have allowed it to be so dominant. One of the main lessons this has driven home is that you constantly need to ask yourself, "Am I doing everything I possibly can be doing to exploit this song?" It's amazing how many additional exploitation opportunities you can find for a song when you think beyond the obvious. From the steps the company takes to connect it's geographically-dispersed staff and roster to ensure that songs are reaching their full potential in international markets to the initiatives the company has launched to revitalize the earning power of the older songs in its catalog, EMIMP is really setting an example in this respect."

"How can artists benefit from publishing deals?"

"Publishers take on three main roles that allow writers to focus on the creative process. First, publishers exploit the songs they represent, meaning they work to place them into income-generating situations (i.e., securing cuts on albums or sync placements). Second, publishers handle administration, meaning they register the songs they represent with the copyright office, as well as with various rights societies, and issue licenses. Third, publishers handle collection, meaning they collect all of the income generated by the songs they represent and distribute the appropriate share to the writers. But that's just the tip of the iceberg. There are countless ways artists can benefit from publishing deals, many of which involve connections. When EMIMP holds a writers' conference, superstar writers like Diddy will be in the same room as the company's newer writers. It gives everyone a chance to network and collaborate with people they would have otherwise never met. Furthermore, an artist will often land a publishing deal before a record deal, and sometimes the artist won't have any team whatsoever when they sign their publishing deal. In such cases, the publisher can be instrumental in helping the artist get signed by a label, or find the right manager, lawyer, or agent by introducing the artist to contacts."

"What is the best way to research music publishing so one feels more comfortable going in? Also, are there any common misconceptions with music publishing?"

"There are some great books out there to start with. Donald Passman's "All You Need to Know About the Music Industry," Eric Beall's "Making Music Make Money," and Mark Halloran's "The Musician's Business and Legal Guide" all come to mind.

"If you're a songwriter, it's a good idea to join a performing rights organization; they often hold educational events for their members. If you're really serious about studying the industry, I strongly recommend looking into the Berklee College of Music's online offerings. You can chose between enrolling in individual courses and enrolling in certificate programs. Soon, you'll even be able to enroll in degree programs. I'm an alumni of the Master Certificate in Music Business program, and what I learned, as well as the relationships I formed with students and faculty, has been invaluable.

"More so than misconceptions, I think there's just an overall lack of knowledge with respect to music publishing, at least among those who are starting out. Everyone has an idea of what labels do, but few people outside of the industry are familiar with the idea of music publishing. If you're interested in a career in the music industry, it's important to thoroughly research all the different sectors to ensure you don't overlook a potential career path that would be perfect for you.

"You must have artists approach you all the time with both music submissions and emails. What are some avoidable mistakes artists make when contacting you?"

"You never know from whom a great music tip will come, so I'm very open to receiving pitches. Even so, I can certainly think of some pet peeves, to which I offer this advice: Don't send an email asking permission to send another email with music. You want to make it as easy as possible for an industry person to listen to you, and this creates an unnecessary step. If you want to send someone your music, just do it. Don't attach MP3s to emails unless explicitly asked to do so. It eats up inbox space, and it can be a pain for an industry person to have to download your music in order to listen to it. I appreciate it when artists upload their songs to a private SoundCloud page and enable downloading from there. That way, I can easily stream their work and, if I like it, choose to download it afterward. Three: Don't send messages that could be confused with spam. Every so often, I'll get a vague "check out my work" message that includes a shady-looking link... sometimes the message will only include the shady-looking link (especially when people contact me on Twitter). These are generally the only times I won't listen to something, as I have no idea if it's a legitimate submission."

"Music blogs have fast become the new tastemakers. I spend much of my time checking out blogs for artists I work with, and it's because I tend to find my new music this way too. I believe the format has surpassed magazines and radio for most music fans. What are your thoughts on the rise of the music blog and where things could go from here?"

"For most hardcore music fans, blogs are the new primary method of music discovery, and an artist that manages to climb up

The Hype Machine's popularity charts is virtually guaranteed to garner industry interest.

"When you consider how influential blogs have become (both to music fans and to the industry), and how blogs are often the very first to believe in and support new artists who later go on to accomplish big things, it only makes sense to me that they should look for ways to capitalize on their taste-making prowess by expanding their activities beyond publication. There are a few blogs that are doing this in some capacity: Neon Gold encompasses both a blog and a record label, and Rollo & Grady encompasses both a blog and a music supervision, licensing, and production company. Even so, there is definitely still room for growth with respect to blogs getting creative and building more comprehensive businesses around the artists they cover."

"What kinds of things should an artist focus on besides gaining exposure for their new release?"

"Before they even consider promoting a release, they need to make sure they have the proper infrastructure in place to retain any potential new fans that such promotion might attract. So many artists start performing and seeking media coverage, yet their websites are totally bare. If someone hears about an artist and is interested enough to look into them further, but the artist doesn't have a full website on which people can learn about their story, consume audio and video, find out when they're playing next, be directed to their social media pages, and sign up for their mailing list, there's a good chance that person is going to forget about the artist. Similarly, before an artist starts playing live, they should come up with a take-home item to hand out at shows (i.e., a card that directs people to their website and a free download).

"It can also be beneficial for artists to explore areas that fall beyond the scope of what they're known for. For example, they could hone their craft and earn some extra income by dedicating time to writing jingles (Mike Foster of Foster the People got his start working as a writer for ad-scoring company Mophonics). It's also important to remember that a lot of the music used in film and television is instrumental, so if an artist is skilled at an instrument, writing and recording instrumental songs could open up some new revenue doors for them.

"Of course, artists should also be networking. Music festivals like SXSW shouldn't be viewed just as performance opportunities, but also as opportunities to take advantage of all the chances to mingle with industry people. Furthermore, I've encountered several artists whose day jobs are related to the music industry (working at a label, publisher, studio, etc.). If this is possible for an artist, it's something worth considering, as working in the industry is perhaps the ultimate way to grow your rolodex."

"Do you find that a lot of artists try to appeal to A&R too early in their development? What are some indications of this?"

"Yes. Sometimes an artist will have a good song, but for whatever reason, they throw together a poorly recorded and produced demo and start pitching it. They need to understand that, in the current climate, companies want to spend as little money on development as possible. If the strength of the song doesn't shine through due to a poor demo, the artist isn't going to get very far. When A&Rs hear a record, they generally need to feel like it's at the level at which it could be on radio right now in order to consider signing the artist.

"A more prominent problem is that many artists start pitching their material before they've generated any buzz. If an artist has an absolutely incredible song, it's possible that will be enough to get A&Rs interested, but in most cases, A&Rs need to see that the artist has built a substantive fan base, is getting their songs into income-generating situations, and is getting media coverage. To use business terminology, artists need to provide a "proof of concept" if they expect a company to feel confident enough to invest in signing them these days. Rather than pitching to labels and publishers straight out of the gate, artists would be better served by perfecting their music and then adopting the mindset of getting out there and generating so much buzz that A&Rs are the ones who come calling, not the other way around."

[173]

INTERVIEW WITH JIM HUGHES
OF WAP PUBLISHING

Jim Hughes is a music licensing expert, music-supervisor at WAP Publishing and founder of IndependentMedia-Pros.com, a network of film composers, bands, sound-designers and post-production professionals. He is constantly searching for music for placements in advertisements and film, and interested artists may contact him through Music XRay. www.musicxray.com/profiles/1006.

"Hi Jim. Welcome to Independent Music Promotions. Please tell us about WAP Publishing and what you do?"

"Hi James, thanks so much for having me. WAP Publishing (http://www.wappublishing.com) is music publishing company that focuses on licensing music to some of the world's leading global brands. We work directly with brands like Microsoft, GM, Sony, Unilever, Coke, Pepsi, Chevy and many others. They express their need for certain styles of music, and we connect them with the artists and songs they are looking for. We work with up-and-coming artists as well as charting "hit" artists in sourcing music for these brands, as well as using our signed artists to create custom compositions whenever the need arises. My particular job is to find new talent for our roster and to find the music that these brands are looking for. I guess you could say I am an A&R for advertising, in a sense."

"You also run the popular www.independentmediapros.com. Please share with us what it is and how it works."

"Over the years, as a composer myself, I have often spent hours "googling" for different avenues to promote and offer my scoring services to the producers who are searching for music. One thing I noticed after a while is that there wasn't really any type of "go-to" directory for film composers. There were a few directories out there, but the listings usually only consisted of a

[174]

short bio and a couple of links maybe. This didn't make any sense to me at all.

"If you are looking for a composer for your film, wouldn't you want to see their film reels, listen to their music, or see what type of work they have done in the past? So I decided to build a website that would include all of that info and more. I created a network where each artist can create their own customized profile, each with a music player, video reel, artwork, bio, credits, and other searchable classifications. Over the last couple of years the site has definitely gained momentum, and I hope that one day it WILL become the website that producers use to find the music professional they need for their project."

"You may have noticed, as have I, that many artists and bands seem stuck on trying to sell CD's the traditional way but mystified as to how licensing (film, TV, games, commercials) works. Is it that complicated, or are artists just not very educated in this aspect of the industry?"

"I don't necessarily think that it is that complicated. I think the main obstacle is that musicians are artists, not lawyers. The world of music licensing is all about contracts, and we all know how devastating those can be, especially in this industry, where the major labels are basically the lawyers and businessmen, and the musicians are the artists and could usually care less about the paperwork until it bites them in the rear."

"What advice would you give musicians who want to get started with the process of licensing their music?"

"The best advice I can give is to read, read, and read again. Get your hands on every music law/business journal, book, or blog that you can find and make yourself read it until you understand it. No one is going to do it for you and this is stuff that you have to know to be successful as an independent musician. Also, you MUST join a performing rights organization (PRO). If you are not a member of a PRO, you aren't going to receive any royalties anyway, so you should do this first and foremost.

"If you're looking to join a PRO outside the U.S., make sure that the rights you assign to them don't restrict either you or your works, specifically the ability to self-administer your performance royalties where appropriate. Also make sure you register your music with Sound Exchange. They are a non-profit organization that collects royalties for streaming services such as satellite radio, internet radio, cable TV streaming music channels and other types of streaming music platforms. If you are outside of the U.S. there are organizations there that do this as well. You can find more detailed information on these topics by reading almost any book about music law or business."

"What are the biggest misconceptions artists may have when it comes to licensing?"

"Many artists feel that just because their music is popular and well produced, that they are automatically going to get the placement. This is definitely not the case. If working in this industry has taught me anything, it is that there is absolutely no telling what a client is going to be looking for in a song. No matter how perfectly you think a song might fit for a particular placement, the vision that the producer has in their mind could be and usually IS completely different. And most importantly, don't let this slow you down or cause you to think your music is worthless.

"With the amount of media in the marketplace right now (mobile content, TV, films, websites, businesses streaming radio, and so on) I can guarantee you that there is someone out there who IS looking for your song. The key is to make sure they can find it. This is the advantage that we now have as independent musicians. We now have access to virtually unlimited free resources to promote our music. Use them! And above all, make sure that they can get in touch with you if they are interested."

"How would someone go about starting a career in music placement?"

"The best resource you can have if you want to get into music licensing is your contact list. Not so much connections with the producers, more so with other musicians. The best thing you can do is build an email database of all the musicians that you connect with on a daily basis. When someone "friends" you on a website, take the time to add their information and email address to your list. Even go so far as to set up different lists for different genres and types of music.

" When a producer is trying to find music for a project, it is most likely that they want to get it from one source if possible. If you can show them that not only can you produce music in your comfort genres, but that you can also easily find any other styles that they might be looking for, they are that much more likely to do business with you."

"What inspires you about the music industry today? What makes you excited to get up in the morning?"

"My excitement definitely springs from the "uncertain" nature of the industry right now. The digital era has opened up a whole new can of worms, and we are now in the middle of a music revolution that is bigger than any before it. It is time to think outside the box and people are starting to realize that there is the now the potential to rise above the masses with new ideas and musical concepts that weren't possible before. We are not just musicians anymore. We are now master promoters, businessmen, and networkers as well and if you're not doing all of these, you're not going to be able to keep up. I can't wait to see how this all unfolds and I hope that the musicians come out on top because they deserve it more than anyone!"

INTERVIEW WITH RADIO HOST JUSTIN WAYNE
(The Justin Wayne Show)

While pursuing careers in everything from film production, video editing, secondary school teaching, s.o.m.a., and commercial radio, Justin Wayne stumbled upon the exciting new medium of podcasting. He now hosts and produces the very popular Justin Wayne Show, a podcast that seeks out the best independent music worldwide and introduces their picks to their listeners. I really respect shows like this that are very open to unsigned artists, but also maintain quality control to gain the trust of their listener-base. Justin is a wealth of knowledge and I was excited to pick his brain in this exclusive interview, asking questions that are most relevant to independent artists and bands.

" Justin, please tell us about The Justin Wayne Show; what its origins were and how it benefits independent artists."

"It all began as a joke that my brother made, and I started a little travel and music blog about five years ago. With a bit of experience in podcasting at a previous job, I started asking unsigned artists if I could add their tunes to a weekly podcast, and it's grown from there over the last four years. We are now active members in the Association of Music Podcasting and have stuck to our guns only playing unsigned and independent artists. We do as much as we can to provide a professional, high quality show with a mix of genres of independent music and I believe that we've found an audience who expects a well-researched show with new music for them to consider purchasing and downloading from the artists."

"How can independent artists properly send their music to podcasts and music blogs? There is a lot of conflicting information out there, and most musicians know there is a good chance their email won't get read in the first place."

"That's a good question and I agree – there is a lot of conflicting information out there. From my own perspective it comes down to one thing: creating relationships. The artists who I am most willing to play on my show aren't necessarily the ones with great tunes – although you've got to have those as well – but the ones who are personable, have a story, and are willing to help promote the show on their end.

"I think artists forget that they bring a little virtual crowd of people with them wherever their music is played, but the people need to know when it's being played and where to go. So: be personal the emails that you send out to shows AND let them know that you're going to help promote the show when you appear. It's attractive to us pod/broadcasters and more fun at the end of the day."

"Please share your thoughts on the controversial issue of free file sharing and its effects on independent artists."

"This isn't a new issue. Cassettes in the 70s and 80s made the record companies worried as well because people were sharing music. Sharing music is the key word there, and usually this is what "free file sharing" is – people passing your music around and talking about it. If they're not buying the album, then they've got that $10 to spend on something else.

"Give them something else to spend that money on. Topspin Media provides a popular direct-to-fan platform for artists and their best selling point is $17. That's way better that $0.99 that is lost when someone downloads the song. The value of a track starts at $0, so it's the artists' job now to find a way to add value to it somehow."

"Is the music industry evolving or collapsing? Does it matter?"

"There will always be music makers and music listeners, so my answer would be that the music industry is evolving – perhaps like a phoenix, but there you go. There are more people listening to more music than ever before, and there's more music available than ever before so in my opinion the music industry is booming with opportunity. However, the "big money music" players as it were are reworking their business models to cope with the new and fast-changing landscape of it and I believe that independent musicians are in the most flexible place to move with the times."

"Many artists don't seem to know how to promote themselves properly. What are some of the most common mistakes you see artists make all the time?"

"I could make a little list for you: BCC emails to tons of people. Don't do this, ever. Start a mailing list, be personal. Sending out bad quality demos to radio – make sure you have excellent material before sending it out. Even if you have to cut back the recordings to acoustic guitar and singing, have an excellent product before you send out to radio.

"Don't get mad at podcasters for not getting back to you right away – many of us are hobbyists or part-timers who are doing this for the love of independent music. We're on your side—we all need to stick together.

"Don't quit. If you want to do this, it IS possible. Make great music, then take an online marketing course or develop your own website blog. Those skills will take you far in this independent music business."

"What inspires you to specifically assist independent musicians the way you do? Do you constantly find new gems?"

"Not constantly, no. I respond to each artist or PR Company who personally submits to try and guide them through some of the mistakes I shared above. I also encourage them to send stuff again later if I didn't accept it for airplay the first time and give them constructive feedback. When I do find gems I do get very excited, especially the ones whom I've told to send better quality stuff back later on. What I love best about this is seeing these artists grow over time."

"Is music more difficult to promote these days? Do you feel the market is oversaturated?"

"Sure, the market is saturated and I would love to say that it's easy to get through to an audience but it's not. So many bands come, go, release, disappear... I believe that the key in the industry right now is consistency. That's what your audience is

[180]

looking for, so give it to them. Keep in constant contact with your fans, give them regular updates and opportunities to see, hear, and buy from you and include them in what you do. Find your fans and give them what they want – ask them what that is!"

"What do you look for in artists you choose to promote?"

"I try to find artists where we can work together. The musicians provide the music and I provide a place for an audience to come and listen. I think that any free-form radio show like this needs a partnership between each artist like any gig – all the artists bring a few people to expose to the other bands. It can be quite fun in the chat room getting bands talking. I also like interesting music and bands that have a story. If a band has a story it's much easier to find something to say about them on the air and people remember those stories. Musicians are storytellers – they can use that skill in their marketing."

"Very few people seem to understand the music industry. Can you leave us with some advice for anyone looking to follow their dreams and make music their career?"

"Unless you end up getting your foot in the door somehow, you're not going to get signed on a major label unless you've got at least 10,000 fans and have a solid social presence on the net. At this point, unless you're a band with a lot of costs, you should be able to sustain yourselves.

"Basically a major label is a band who may (or many not) be willing to invest in you. They're smart about this, and give you about ten per cent of the profit, which also has to pay for your production costs. The math has never added up for me, nor many who have been in the music industry. There's a book by Jacob Slichter, the drummer of Semisonic, called "So You Wanna Be a Rock and Roll Star" which I highly recommend. I also recommend finding someone internet and business savvy to work with your band instead, create your own record label, and do your best on your own. If nothing else, it'll get you noticed by a major at some stage."

"Lastly, please give us the scoop on how we can tune in to the Justin Wayne Show."

[181]

"We've been doing live broadcasts completely independent of any station directly from http://thejustinwayneshow.com and it looks like we're going to be expanding in the near future. We're live every Monday at 12pm PST, 3pm EST, 8pm GMT and always podcasted the following Wednesday. Two-hours of independent music each week including rock, pop, acoustic, indie, live features and free downloads. Artists can submit directly to http://thejustinwayneshow.com/submitmusic and we also have a very active account on MusicXray.

INTERVIEW WITH CRYSTAL LEE OF VANDALA CONCEPTS

Crystal Lee is the CEO of Vandala Concepts, a very ambitious company offering just about every service you could imagine to independent artists, not to mention a magazine, and she has the industry knowledge to make it all effective.

"Crystal, please tell us about Vandala Concepts, how you got started with it and what you offer independent artists."

"I got started many years ago when I was fifteen, and by luck in the modeling/dance world. Some may disagree but it's a form of entertainment. I learned contracts and the nasty ones at that. I stayed with modeling since it paid better, although I have always had my foot in music. I was classically trained on the flute and piccolo. Yes, make the American pie jokes all you want but the flute/piccolos are evil little beasts; they take a lot of technique, ear training and more. Being part of an honors wind ensemble band taught me so much such as listening, tuning, scales and theory, etc. Though, again, I am a rocker at heart.

"I grew up with all types of music; country, metal, classic rock, eighties music (sadly, my mother loved it). I love music and it has always been a huge part of my life - period. I write lyrics, poetry, and the occasional song. Again, not the right fit even with being published in over two hundred poetry anthologies by the age of nineteen. I knew I would be a starving artist and it wasn't my calling. Music was, but not as a singer.

"By nineteen, I was working for a major label part time (University the other part) for a few years and became the devil, learned what I could and left the company since I was brought up with morals and ethics. Not only did the bands I worked with sell their soul - mine died a little. Also, I heard my grandmothers'

[183]

voice of morals in my head like Jiminy Cricket. I always continued with bookings and working with indie bands on the side but never could take the jump to run my own business fully. But I just wanted to make a difference in the indie scene and help bands achieve their dreams. Talent is talent and it should be seen.

"For years I worked full time jobs and worked part time in the music industry because it was scary to give up that stable pay check and become self-employed. In 2006 I became a certified event and talent manager because it was paid for by the government since they believed in me and thought what I was doing on the side was great. Honestly, I would never have gone back for any school unless I was paid to do so. While in school, I was able to intern with Doc Robertson, Music Director and a full fold out card of other jobs at Sun FM Kelowna. I showed up and said I need to know more about radio since that was a weakness. He taught me so much and had faith in me personally, career wise and showed me the right side of the industry. I gained experience over many years in so many areas and did so many things but it was all for a reason. I needed to learn certain lessons in life and skills which I needed to be successful in the music industry. By 2009, my now husband said you are burning the candle stick at both ends and need to take the jump, get serious and work in the music industry. I did. I needed the right person to give me the push. He also said I could do more if I gave more time. He was right. Shhhh…don't tell him that.

"It all started with one marketing plan and ended up here today with a few 360's. Adaptability keeps you in the industry. 2012 has been the explosion year though. Magazine, music services, six staff and little sleep. One thing still remains; Dedication, Trust, and Passion in the Industry. I may not be the number one person or magazine in the industry right now but I can guarantee you that I am dedicated to my clients, and artists I work with and that are in our magazine. I also take great pride that artists can trust Vandala and most of all that we see their passion. I am lit up by that and thus my passion and love for the independent scene makes me give one hundred and ten per cent.

The magazine formed itself, really. Smaller bands do not always get the press and require some press so I created a newsletter and somewhere over the years it's grown into a magazine all by itself. It is a publication that does not follow the rules and has the goal of bringing the best music to light and artists that you should hear. Most of all, we publish the positive; if negative, it's in a way to bring light to a problem; if you want to hear the negative turn on the media. Some disagree but I believe not getting reviews, plays, hits and more is an obvious sign for a band that something is wrong. Also, contact people for help and opinions. We live in a world there are enough people out there willing to tell you where you need to improve, and maybe some too willing."

"What are some of the most common mistakes you see independent artists make?"

"You had to go there! They make a lot of mistakes and do not realize it. Yes, there are the basics but I will give you a few that I see too often and should not see:

"Email basics and mass emails! Lately, that alone drives me nuts. Email Etiquette for one - pick up a cheap book on emailing.

"Next, no mass emails: so many do not even BCC it. It's like the guy you see hitting on every girl at the bar. Not only does he look desperate, he looks like so many things I'd rather not say, though most likely that guy gets slapped but in email delete and block. If you cannot take the time why should I?

"Artists not realizing how many emails I get...I get so many. With a magazine and services, it opens up many doors to be contacted.

"Not picking up the phone at all! Wait a minute, this does not mean to call me like a crazy girlfriend. Pick up the phone, follow up, and ask questions and so forth. Email first then call ideally. When someone calls me, they become a real person and not another email. Again, it may be rude but its reality: it's so much easier for me to get you where you want to go. It's instant and personal. Also, with services I can do so much more over the phone, such as figure out what you really need, and what is a waste. Most of all I will remember you more because you are not just another email.

"Know who you are dealing with. If Vandala magazine is interviewing, you go read it, and see what writer you're dealing with. Also, before you contact me, go to my site and see what we do. I get emails from people asking me to play their music on my radio station???? We are not one. You just look bad when you do things like that. Go to all sites and find out as much as you can, such as what they do, genres they accept etc. Also, again, it's a respect thing.

"Not following the rules – if there are guidelines, follow them. If they say digital downloads, no large files, or fill out the form, they mean it. You get deleted when you do not follow the requirements generally. Great talent still needs to read and follow the requirements. In two days, I had over eight hundred emails in one email account, and guess what the guys who did not follow the guidelines got deleted to get the email amount down. If you think about it, isn't it disrespectful to not take the time?

"We give you an amazing review and you delete yourself off our mailing list, ouch. Join and ditch does not make a nice impression. In a way, it's a shallow move and you won't get another review. I hate to say but I have a list of bands that really mess up, and this includes other professionals as well. Don't burn your bridges since it's a small industry and it's viral.

"Social Media – use it and use it properly. Gong shows online are still gong shows. Keep the personal drama off the web, never talk shit, since again, you could burn bridges. Also, Twitter, Facebook, and all the other social media...be on it and be interesting. I also note that Facebook and Twitter are different, so use them the right way. Most of all, blog. Bands who are interesting keep a fan base while making albums. If you're touring then tweet, post pictures, etc. People in the Facebook age even post their lunch. Sad, but its true, so use it to your advantage.

"Contact Info – always have that easy to find. If I cannot contact you how can I do anything for you?

[186]

"Have a Proper website. Myspace and Facebook are not band websites. They are social media. There is Wordpress, too, if you're on a budget. Look serious, or I won't take you serious."

"What are some of the qualities you look for in an artist?"

"Constantly Active, Passion, Seriousness, Professionalism, Respect, Trust. They must have DIY abilities and no drama. Also, they must have the "it" factor. Yes, a cliché but its real. Some guys come off cocky, arrogant, and fake while the real talent comes off passionate, dedicated and just a true talent. This is the guy you can't help but watch even if he has lower skills, and thus he is someone you can work with. Most of all, be a long term talent. You can always give someone lessons to improve their skills but you can't make the "it" factor."

"What are the characteristics of a great press/news release?"

"This might be a controversial one here for me, but I am blunt and tell it how it is for me:

"First of all, use a legible font. I need to be able to read it. That goes for tour posters, event posters, band logos etc. If I can't read it I delete it.

"Have all the links there, your bands site, social media, etc where I can hear your music. I hate it when the only link I see is the publicists. Who cares about the publicist (I am one and I am not important - the artist is). It's our job to promote the band. Also, make it easy for me. I have limited amount of time. I do not want to jump through hoops to get what I need. Again, delete is so easy these days.

"Edit: large indie labels have sent me stuff that has needed drastic editing. Read and re-read. It sucks but it has to be done.

"This might be a controversial one here for me, since I have been breaking the rules on Press releases, but for us it's about being interesting and showing the talent. Vandala has its own style that is not boring and uses it to stand out at times. Yes, you have the APA style that has all the information. This is great to some but when I see hundreds you do need to stand out some. That also goes for anything you send anyone. Again when people see hundreds of something everything starts to look the same an even blurry. Be it a photo, great start up line or Title. Think about it from my end; hundreds of emails of the same thing, so what would you do?"

"You offer radio promotion. Are there any public misconceptions about what this entails?"

"I think all the services are sometimes misconceived mainly on how much work we put in on the business side. I have talked to many people in the industry and the common comments are the amount of time we put in into a campaign is not realized, be it in publicity, radio tracking, and more, which lead to so many assuming we over charge. Look at our hourly rate then make the comments. It all takes time and effort. With radio tracking we do tracking for campus and indie radio in Canada. This entails calling every radio station, making a kick ass package, strong relationships and constant follow up. We call and email for weeks and it takes hours of work. This also goes for your publicity, contract/agreement writing, and all our services."

"Some of your services involve documentation preparation and review. I think many bands miss out on opportunities simply because they're afraid of contracts of any kind. What has your experience been and can you please tell us more about what this service entails?"

"This means any paper work, or more often digital paper work such as Press Kits, EPK's, Media packages, Digital Creations, Portfolios, copywriting and more. Also, we review things like contracts, agreements, licensing deals, grant applications, and whatever else comes your way in the industry. One thing we do is review contracts from the industry bands receive. I may not be a lawyer but I am way cheaper. Also, if you need a lawyer I will tell you. I used to be on the other end, but now I am fighting for bands to get the best deals and every penny counts.

"Contracts and agreements can be scary. If you have ever signed a loan, it's a serious commitment and is terrifying but agreements are part of our everyday lives. If nothing else, there is terms and services you agree to even Facebook. So yes, bands are at times afraid but it comes down to having the right people and team to help you. An agreement puts it on paper of what each party is going to do and lays out the terms such as pay, length, what happens if the agreement is broken etc. Bookings, producer contracts, to label agreements I would never do anything serious without an agreement because as "House says everyone lies" sadly it happens in this industry too much and in the rest of the world. Think about it. Does a bank give you a credit card without an agreement?

"Also, when it's a large contract, like a label one, I tell bands that each member should look at it and anyone else they can get to look at it, even your grandmother. I have also taken all the highlighted copies and put them together with the issues, questions, and concerns. Make a list of questions and then go see a lawyer if possible. Entertainment lawyers are extremely expensive, and why waste money if you do not have to with extra hours sitting with them? Be prepared when you go see a lawyer and remember hundreds of dollars an hour is what you are going pay, though think about what a bad deal will cost you in the long run.

"The other aspect is we negotiate agreements for artists as well. Sometimes when I come in, things work a little faster and better. Not all artists know the business world and that's okay, we all have our strengths. Never be afraid to ask for help on agreements and contracts. We also even have standard ones I can draw up for a band within the hour."

"In my experience, most independent artists seem to do things one after the other without a sense of timing or urgency. They release an album, start promoting it two weeks later, then plan a video, contact some radio shows and maybe book a few live dates. Can you share your perspective on the ideal overall structure of an album promotion campaign and the importance of its timing?"

"Again, if it's not urgent to you it won't be urgent to me. Album promotion campaigns do not happen overnight, nor do any campaign. Each company is different and for us we require a

[189]

minimum of four to six weeks before the album is released. If you want more such as reviews, tour and promo, then we may need more time. We are only human. Promotion is an art, and has to be done right as it's a competitive market. The early bird gets the worm literally. Doing both promotions and having a magazine has showed me so much. The magazine is a month or two ahead in some areas, so showing up last minute won't be successful at our magazine.

"Also, artists have to have a full plan. Release, tour dates, videos and so forth have to be done in the right time frame and right way. Think of a campaign as waves. You have to keep it going and know where, how and when, you're going to get there - otherwise you're dead on the beach. Also, if you have a plan you can save money by doing some things all at once such as radio tracking and album release at the same time. Most of all you will have greater success with a plan. You band is a business! Treat it as such. It's a known fact businesses without marketing plans are more likely to fail. That goes for your band as well. It's obvious the bands who work and the bands without a plan because you see the reviews, sales, hits and attention. Serious bands plan and take the time to do it right."

"There seem to be a lot of independent artists with major grievances out there, and one thing I notice is that they end up sharing their complaints on forums and blogs, while other artists tour and work hard. What's the perspective of the successful artist as opposed to the bitter one?"

"Once on the net it's there forever, and remember that everyone is watching for drama. We live in a world of reality TV; this drama has taken over and it becomes a virus. Before talking negatively think about these things: Is this a hurt ego or legit? What will I gain? What will I lose? Do I look stupid? Is it worth it? What connections do they have? Who is watching? - If I am, I will delete you along with the drama!

"There are professional ways to deal with things and publicly and on the net is not the way. If you do leave the names out and be editorial about it, make a point about what the problem is in a professional way. Also ask and try to work it out especially with the emailing and texting, real meanings get lost fast and assumptions happen too often.

"As for bitterness, yes we all have it and no one is alone. Have a support system. I won't lie. I have it some days, but I get over it. Working hard and being successful is the best way to deal with it. Also, never ask why. You may think this is out there but this concept changed my life and literally saved it. You only ask why about a scientific process. Otherwise, you don't really want the answer to the question why. For example, a girlfriend calls and asks why didn't you do this? Why, why, why? The reality is that she wants a fight, not an answer. If she calls up and says "What happened?" you will respond in a positive way and not a defensive way. So, in the industry you ask what went wrong, when did this happen and how do I fix this? Where do I go from here, and so on. "Why" can be a form of self-destruction and holds you back."

"Anything you'd like to add?"

"Work hard, treat your band as a business, dust, yourself off, and grow a thick skin. Life is hard and this industry is no different. Remember though, there are good people out there to help. Vandala is here. Most of all play for the love, not the money, because when you are old and gray that guitar may be your best friend.

"Also, the biggest teacher and inspiration now is my daughter. She likes what she likes, does what she does to be happy. Carefree, confident and she keeps it simple. As we grow older, we lose those things. She likes what music she likes with no care for anyone else's opinion or push. Even if you did push, any song she will cry to is what she does not like. With the media pushing things on us, a six month old child is the one doing it right – being who she really is.

[191]

_____IN CLOSING_____

You are guaranteed to get results when you put honest, professional, and unrelenting work into the promotion of your music. The results will depend on how good you are, how neutral you are, and how hard you work. I wish you the best, and hope you get in touch with your success stories and feedback, and remember, your band is a virus!

Contact James Moore through his website at www.independentmusicpromotions.com.

CPSIA information can be obtained at www.ICGtesting.com
Printed in the USA
LVOW04s1852120115

422514LV00035B/2418/P